Problem Dog

VALERIE O'FARRELL

Problem Dog
Behaviour and Misbehaviour

GUILD PUBLISHING
LONDON · NEW YORK · SYDNEY · TORONTO

This edition published 1989 by
Guild Publishing by arrangement with
Methuen London Ltd

Copyright © Valerie O'Farrell 1989

CN 2078

Printed and bound in Great Britain by
Butler & Tanner Ltd, Frome, Somerset

Contents

Acknowledgments

I should like to offer my grateful thanks to the following:

Dr Peter Darke, Director of the Small Animal Clinic, and the late Professor James Baxter of the Department of Veterinary Medicine, Edinburgh University, for enabling me to work there at a time when many vets regarded dog psychologists with suspicion.

Gillian Jordan, for urging me to write this book.

My father, Nigel Walker, for his help, particularly for reading and commenting on early drafts of the typescript.

Jane Gough, for her speedy and efficient typing.

Ann Mansbridge of Methuen, for being such a sympathetic and encouraging editor.

My husband Paul and my daughters Margaret and Katharine, for all their support and help.

Lastly, I would like to thank all the owners and their dogs without whom this book could not have been written.

Illustrations are by Moira Chesmur; those on page 56 and page 59, below, are reproduced by kind permission of Pedigree Petfoods.

Introduction

This is a book on canine psychology: about how a dog's mind works.

Its main aim is to help owners whose dogs' behaviour presents a problem, but I hope it will also be interesting to other dog owners, as well as to the general reader who would like to know more about dogs. Clearer insight into why your dog acts as he does can enrich your relationship with him. It can also help to prevent problems.

Most books about dogs are written by 'doggy' people: people who have been brought up with dogs and who have lived with dozens of them. What they write is based on this experience. This book is different; it is not a 'doggy' book but a scientific one. I am not a 'doggy' person; I am fond of dogs, I am a dog owner, but I was not brought up with them: I have lived on intimate terms with only a few.

I am a psychologist and it is as a psychologist that I have written this book. At the University of Edinburgh I run a clinic for problem dogs, who are referred to me by their vets. An owner brings his dog, we discuss the problem in detail and I hope to advise him as to how best to deal with it. A great deal of this advice is based on fairly straightforward psychological principles. My aim in this book is to make these directly accessible to the reader, so that he can carry out his own diagnosis and treatment.

The first part of the book deals mostly with various areas of dog psychology; Chapter 7 deals with owner psychology. It also explains how problems can arise. Part II is practical. Chapters 8 to 11 are a step-by-step guide to diagnosis and treatment. Chapter 12 deals with prevention.

The problem dogs described in this book are all real cases. Inessential details have been altered, in order to protect the anonymity of the owners.

Part I
How a Dog's Mind Works

1 • *What Is a Problem Dog?*

A smartly dressed woman in her forties was towed into my consulting room by a large red setter. She sat down, as invited, but the dog lunged here and there barking at the end of his lead: trying to jump up on me, trying to explore the room, trying to get out the way he had come. She shouted 'Sit' and 'Bad boy' at him, without much conviction and certainly without any effect. I suggested she let him off his lead, whereupon he sniffed at me, rummaged in the wastepaper basket, tried to look out of the window and finally lifted his leg on a cupboard door. As he gradually calmed down, I heard from the owner, Mrs Rutherford, about life with Rollo.

He was about two years old; she and her husband had acquired him a year before from an elderly couple who 'couldn't manage him'. They had owned trouble-free dogs previously and had thought that exercise and some training would put matters right. They were mistaken. Rollo spent most of his waking hours cruising round the house looking for excitement. Any noise, such as voices outside, birds or the telephone, was enough to trigger off a fit of barking. Cats were his special interest. Unfortunately the Rutherfords owned two elderly ones: Rollo had recently managed to catch the less agile of them and toss it in the air. Now the cats spent most of the day outside. Mrs Rutherford spent much of the day making sure that cats and dog never met. She shut the dog in the garden while the cats had their breakfast in the kitchen. She held on to the dog's collar while she escorted the cats out again, and so on. When there was nothing exciting going on, Rollo turned to his owners for attention, whining and pawing at them until they patted him. Though Rollo was tiring to be with, the consequences of leaving him on his own were even worse. In the house, he was liable to scratch the paintwork of doors closed against him and chew up loose objects such as books or cushions. Left in the car, he could do even more expensive damage, making short work of the seats and interior.

Mrs Rutherford was clearly at her wits' end with Rollo; tears came to her eyes as she talked of her dilemma. He had never harmed anyone, indeed was an extremely loving and affectionate dog, but life with him was impossible.

The reaction of many people to Mrs Rutherford's predicament is probably one of pity mingled with scorn. The scorn is perhaps partly a reflection of the British revulsion against consulting a psychiatrist or psychologist. To consult one about one's own difficulties is bad enough, but if you consult one about a dog you must be really crazy. There is also the commonly held view that 'there are no bad dogs, only bad owners'. If someone has a problem dog it must be his own fault.

Unfortunately, this is a myth. There are plenty of dogs on the market who are potential trouble looking for a place to happen. That place could be the home of any nice, ordinary, unsuspecting dog lover. By the time an owner acquires a puppy, its personality is already partly formed and may contain the seeds of problem behaviour.

For example, there is little doubt that Rollo was to some extent the victim of his genes. Some breeds, such as red setters, are notoriously exuberant and hard to control. And if a behavioural tendency is commoner in one breed than another, then the chances are it is to some extent genetically determined. Also, the fact that Rollo had been passed from one owner to another probably did him no good. Being destructive when left alone is a stress reaction and it is more often seen in dogs with unsettled early lives.

Of course the way the owners behave towards a dog also has a great influence on its behaviour and much of this book is concerned with explaining how owners can exert this influence for the better. But it must always be borne in mind that there are some dogs who, by virtue of their inheritance and early environment, would present a problem to any owner. Conversely, of course, there are some owners who are unfit to own a dog. Many people may still feel that, even if they had the bad luck to be landed with a dog like Rollo, they would not allow him to disrupt their lives in the way Mrs Rutherford did. Some may be convinced that they would be able to quell him by the force of their personalities; they 'wouldn't stand any nonsense'. Others may think they simply would not tolerate such a dog in the house: he would have to be destroyed. There are people of this kind, who simply do not allow a problem like this to occur, but it is worth bearing in mind that it is much easier to see a solution to a problem when you are standing outside it. People who have never had a problem dog of their own often cannot really visualize what it is like. 'Not standing any nonsense' is usually easier to recommend than to do. Also, it may be possible to contemplate getting rid of a 'problem dog' in the abstract, but when that dog rushes to greet you when you come home or comes up and lays his head in your lap when you sit down in the evening, it may be a completely different matter.

Nowadays, it is not socially acceptable to be superior about people in difficulties. We do not go down to Bedlam to laugh at the lunatics; we do not consider that physical disability is a sign of God's displeasure. But in Britain, at any rate, it is still considered shameful to have a problem dog; the owners themselves usually feel ashamed too.

If you look around, you constantly see owners desperately struggling to make their dog present a socially acceptable face to the world. The parks are full of owners calling dogs' names with no dog in sight and dogs trotting around with no visible owner. They are full of owners towed along by dogs straining on leashes. Why are those dogs on leads? Not because dog or owner enjoys taking walks that way, but because if he is off the lead, he is liable to do something embarrassing. If you ring someone's doorbell, it is fairly common to have to wait a few minutes listening to barks and shouts and scuffling while a protesting dog is bundled into the kitchen. Alternatively, if the owner has decided on a 'free-range' policy, you can often sense her stiffen with anxiety as he comes to greet you, for fear of what he may do.

These observations lead one to the conclusion that although as a nation we maintain the fiction that problem dogs are unBritish, in fact they are very common. It is just that their owners keep very quiet about them. This conclusion is supported by research findings. An American survey of dog owners carried out by telephone found that, although most owners were fond of their dogs and regarded them as members of the family, for twenty-five per cent of owners the dog was more of a worry than a pleasure, because of its behaviour.

I found a similar proportion in a smaller survey of my own of fifty randomly selected Edinburgh dog owners. Ten of these dogs, one in five, had behaviour problems that caused the owners serious inconvenience. These included habits like constantly urinating or defecating in the house, biting anyone who came near him when he was eating or barking whenever the television was turned on. In addition, another thirty dogs had more minor problems, which nevertheless caused some inconvenience. These included dogs who jumped up on visitors or, on a walk, ate any rubbish they could find or did not come when they were called. Only one owner in five felt he had a perfectly behaved dog.

There was another finding which particularly interested me as an animal behaviour consultant working in conjunction with veterinary surgeons. The owners of problem dogs might have discussed their difficulties with friends, they might have taken their dogs to obedience classes, but none of them had talked to their vets about the problem. Perhaps this is not so surprising, as most people expect their vets to treat only physical problems and indeed until recently vets have had little to offer other than advice gleaned from their own experience.

Several years ago, before I was involved in animal behaviour problems on a professional basis, a friend told me of an experience which deeply impressed me. She had a dog who developed a habit of urinating on the beds. It happened in one particular situation only: when someone went upstairs to have a bath. If she could, the dog would sneak up behind the person and on to the bed. At any other time she could be trusted in the bedrooms with perfect safety. A rule was laid down in the household that anyone who had a bath had to be sure to keep his bedroom door shut, but of course every now and again someone forgot. This is the kind of problem which, every time it occurs, occurs once too often: it is no joke trying to wash dog urine out of a duvet. In desperation, my friend decided to try her vet. He was a kindly old chap, but she felt a bit awkward about the whole thing, so she tried to mention it casually during a consultation about something else. She knew immediately she started that it was a mistake. The atmosphere of embarrassment between them grew as she floundered on through the whole rigmarole about baths and shutting bedroom doors. She began to feel she lived in a mad household of which this crazy dog was just one manifestation. When she had finished, the poor man silently thrust at her a leaflet, put out by one of the pet food companies, entitled 'How to house-train your puppy'. They both knew that the dog was certainly no puppy and it did not seem to be a problem of house-training exactly, but she accepted the leaflet as a way out of an awkward situation. Neither of them ever referred to the matter again.

Since I became professionally involved with animal behaviour problems, I have talked to vets about how they feel when clients ask them about their dogs' behaviour. I realize now that the awkwardness of my friend's vet probably did not spring from embarrassment over her domestic revelations but merely from a realization that she was in difficulties for which he had nothing to offer her.

Since then, things have changed radically. Most vets now realize that there is a body of scientific knowledge which can help with behaviour problems. The idea first started in America about ten years ago. As long ago as the 1920s, psychologists, interested in how human beings and animals learn, were performing an enormous number of psychological experiments on animals. They were concerned with all kinds of learning: how normal behaviour, such as using language, driving a car or (in a rat's case) running a maze, is learnt; how abnormal behaviour, such as agoraphobia or compulsive checking, is learnt. In the 1960s, out of this body of work emerged techniques which were used to help human psychiatric patients. These techniques are known collectively as 'behaviour therapy'. But it was only about ten years ago that it was realized that such techniques could be successfully applied to the treatment of behaviour disorders in the species of animals on which they were originally developed.

Some of these experiments, for example those in which rats ran mazes for a food reward, were innocuous enough. Others must have caused considerable distress to the animals involved. In one famous experiment, an American psychologist, Masserman, found he could induce neurosis in cats. He taught them to expect food in a certain place; then, when they approached their food bowls, a blast of air was blown in their faces. They retreated in terror to the far end of their cages and refused to approach their food bowls again. Although experiments of this kind seem ethically dubious, to say the least, they will be described and discussed later in this book. This does not imply approval, but what has been done cannot be undone; at least the sufferings of animals now dead can be given a chance to benefit the living.

In addition to 'learning theory', animal behaviour specialists began to make use of other branches of psychology as well. In the 1940s, zoologists such as Konrad Lorenz began to study the instinctive behaviour patterns of animals; they began to puzzle out how animals manage to communicate with each other or carry out such complex tasks as rearing their young without apparently ever having learnt how to do it in the way we have to learn. This kind of study highlighted the complexity and subtlety of these instinctive behaviour systems; also how different they are from our own. When dogs and their wild ancestors, wolves, were studied in this way, it became clear that some of their 'body-language' is not at all the same as ours. One result of this difference is that behaviour problems arise simply because of misunderstandings and miscommunication.

Another branch of psychology which can help with behaviour problems is developmental psychology. Because the dog is such an amenable animal it has been used as a subject in research to find out the ways in which the experience of a young animal can affect its personality as an adult. Interest in the personality of puppies has also come from another quarter. Organizations that train guide dogs spend a great deal of money on each dog: any puppy that is bred and reared by them, but turns out not to be suitable as a guide dog when it grows up, is a wasted investment. These organizations have sponsored research on the best kind of upbringing for a guide-dog puppy. How much human contact does it need? When should it leave its litter-mates?

Pet dogs and their owners can also benefit from this research. We can now be more definite about the effect of puppy upbringing on the adult dog than we can about the effect of different methods of child-rearing. This knowledge can be used to help with behaviour problems: not to treat them, but to prevent them.

Finally, animal psychologists are only just beginning to realize that in order to treat dogs they need to know something about owner psychology too. Most owners know how closely their dogs observe them (many of them have not much else to do) and how sensitive their dogs are to their moods. It is not a surprising idea to most owners, therefore, that dogs are affected not only by their owners' deliberate actions, like rewarding them with tit-bits or shouting at them, but also by owners' attitudes and anxieties of which they are not so clearly aware. This is one of the most fascinating aspects of work with dog behaviour problems. The more cases I see, the clearer it becomes to me that much of a dog's behaviour is closely linked to such things as the owner's feelings about the dog, or the interactions going on in the rest of the family. Often shifts in family atmosphere produce a change for the better or worse in the dog's behaviour; sometimes I can only guess as to how this came about. Obviously the state of our knowledge about the relationship between dogs and their owners is still far from complete.

The main aim of this book is to set out the knowledge of dog psychology so far available in such a way that owners can make use of it. Some owners may wonder how this information differs from the kind of thing they are taught at obedience classes or the kind of advice a 'doggy' friend might give them. Certainly, people who have been brought up with dogs or have worked with them for a long time may develop techniques of handling them which are highly successful. The best dog handlers understand a dog's body language and communicate with him intuitively; these people are fascinating to watch. But most of them do not know why they are so successful; they cannot articulate the principles underlying what they do. If you try to imitate one of these handlers, you may be lucky enough to reproduce the essential features of his behaviour; or you may not. Many clients have described to me the galling experience of going to an obedience class with a rather unruly dog; the dog has made some kind of disturbance, maybe leaping about or barking, and the teacher has taken charge of him. In the teacher's hands, he has behaved like a lamb, sitting on command and so on. But when the teacher gives him back to his owner, he is as bad as ever; when the owner says 'Sit' in a new, fierce voice, the dog just looks at him blankly.

This embarrassing refusal of the dog to obey its owner may be partly due to the fact that his relationships to his handler and to his owner are different. Most of us will do things like stand in a queue or take off our clothes if a man in uniform or a nurse tells us to, but we would look with incredulity at a member of our family who tried to order us about in the same way. An alternative explanation of the dog's refusal may be that the owner has not imitated the essential features of the handler's behaviour. The handler cannot tell him what these essential features are, because he does not know himself.

Another reason why scientifically based principles are more powerful tools for solving dog behaviour problems than personal experience is that, however experienced the trainer, he is limited to the dogs he himself has dealt with. If you ask him what to do about the fact that your dog is liable to get excited in the car and jump about, he will think of other dogs he has known who have done the same thing and of the remedies which worked with them. The trouble is that those other dogs may have been excited for different reasons; therefore the remedy which worked in their case may not work in yours. On the other hand, if you know about the theory of why animals get excited and of how they learn to associate excitement with particular situations, you are much more likely to be able to work out the reasons for your particular dog's behaviour and devise a remedy for it.

Up till now, animal behaviour consultants have worked mostly through vets. There are good reasons for this. In some cases, there may be physical factors involved in a behaviour problem. A dog may be particularly irritable and snappy because his ears hurt; he may start defecating in the house because he has a gastro-intestinal infection. In these cases, it is obviously essential that the medical conditions be diagnosed and treated. Also, in the treatment of some behaviour disorders, drugs may be useful as a temporary aid: to make the dog calmer, for example. So most animal behaviourists accept referrals only from a vet.

In addition, some vets may treat the problem themselves. Although dog behaviour is a standard part of the curriculum in only one British veterinary school, it is possible for vets to gain some expertise through reading books on the subject and through attending lectures and post-graduate courses. Instead of being a bit of a joke and a subject in which only eccentrics took an interest, the topic is rapidly becoming respectable and the level of expertise among vets is steadily increasing. This seems to have happened partly because this expertise meets a need; there is a market for it. It has happened also partly because of the general climate of opinion which has produced concern for such things as animal rights and the preservation of wildlife. These concerns seem to reflect a more prevalent moral view that animals have a right to their own life-styles and living space, that they do not exist simply to be of use to man. This in its turn means that more owners are prepared to take trouble to live on good terms with their pets, including their dogs; that fewer take the view that if a dog does not fit in with their life-style it should be replaced with a more satisfactory model. It also means that owners who want to take the trouble to treat behaviour problems are taken more seriously, particularly by their vets; they are not so likely to be dismissed as soppy or over-involved with their pet.

If your dog has a behaviour problem, therefore, you may well wish to consult your vet about it. He might offer some advice himself, particularly if he is one of the vets who has taken an interest in the subject. Alternatively, he may refer you to an animal behaviourist.

On the other hand, to understand the psychological principles which underly the treatment, you do not have to be a vet. There is no reason why owners should not themselves apply them directly. Some cases, of course, will require veterinary help and some will require psychological help. But there are many behaviour problems, particularly the more minor and straightforward ones, which could be diagnosed and treated by the informed owner by himself. The aim of the rest of the book is to give him the necessary information.

2 • *How a Dog Thinks*

Every species of animal has a brain which works slightly differently from another species and sense organs which send slightly different information to it. This means that although we all inhabit the same physical world, we inhabit different psychological worlds. This is obvious in the case of, say, man and the goldfish. The goldfish may live in the same living-room as us, but he sees it through water and the wall of a glass tank. He does not seem to hear the telephone or smell bacon frying. A worm dropped into the tank is more interesting to him than Aunty Rita paying a visit or a television programme. The fact that a goldfish does not sleep and the fact that it does not seem to get attached to anyone, even another goldfish, makes it hard even to visualize what being a goldfish is like.

In the case of a dog, this identification is much easier. He takes notice of many of the same things which concern us: Aunty Rita, food cooking, the telephone ringing, even an exciting programme on television (especially if it involves animals making a noise), are all things which interest him. It seems fairly easy to tell when he is angry, afraid, loving or happy. But this makes it much harder for us to appreciate that his psychological world is different from ours: not as different as that of the goldfish, but still different. This chapter will examine these differences between a dog's perception of the world and our perception of it. It will also look at intellectual differences: what we make of what we perceive.

Where the senses of hearing and smell are concerned, we are profoundly disabled, in comparison with dogs.

A dog's hearing is much more acute than ours. For example, a sound which is audible to a dog a quarter of a mile away would have to be a hundred yards away to be audible to a person. What is more, a dog can hear high-pitched sounds which are inaudible to us. The highest sound we can hear is about 20,000 cycles per second: dogs can hear sounds of at least 35,000 cycles per second. This is the basis of the 'silent' dog whistle.

In practical terms, this means that through his ears a dog can gather a great deal of information which is lost to us. He can hear members of the family coming home before we can hear them and he can tell one person's footstep from another's. He can also hear intruders and other untoward household happenings of which we are unaware.

The difference between the dog's and the human sense of smell is even greater. It has been estimated that a dog's sense of smell is up to one million times better than man's. This of course is what makes dogs so useful as tracker and sniffer dogs. For pet dogs, it means that whole areas of interest are available to them which are mysteries to us. For example, when we go out for a walk, a great deal of the pleasure for us is in looking around. A dog enjoys that too, but it is clear that he derives even more gratification from all the new smells. For him, the smells are the scenery.

The superior sense of hearing may explain some of the instances of 'pre-cognition' or 'telepathy' in dogs who predict the arrival of their owners or, more dramatically and more usefully, predict disasters such as the collapse of a building. In the same way, it is possible that the acute sense of smell explains accounts of a dog 'knowing' that an unpleasant incident has occurred at a certain spot or that some person is up to no good; dogs can certainly make sense of human odours. On the other hand, it is likely that many of these reactions are based on a dog's expert observation of human body language.

Unlike hearing and smell, a dog's vision is no better or worse than ours, but it is different. This difference is due to the kind of receptive cells to be found in the retina, the sensitive part of the eye on to which the lens projects images of the outside world. Both a human and a canine retina have two kinds of cells: rods and cones. But the proportion of the two kinds differs between the species. A dog has more rods and fewer cones than we do. Cones are sensitive to colour and operate best in daylight. Rods, on the other hand, register only shades of grey and work best at night. So a dog sees better than we do at night, but less well during the day. He has trouble in making out fine detail, especially at a distance, and he relies on things at a distance moving to catch his attention. If your dog runs away from you on a walk, he may not immediately recognize you by sight at a distance. He may even make the embarrassing mistake of running up to someone else, only to discover his mistake when he is quite close. But if you call out to him, he will not make that mistake.

These are generalizations about dogs as a species, but individual dogs and breeds of dogs differ greatly in the use they make of their sensory powers. Some dogs, such as bloodhounds, are particularly good at smelling. When they are tracking they keep their noses to the ground and pay comparatively little attention to sights or sounds. Others, such as greyhounds or Afghans (the 'gazehounds'), rely more on vision: it is the sight of prey running which arouses their hunting instincts.

But the major differences between a dog's psychological world and ours are not due to variations in sensory input. The psychological worlds of deaf people and blind people have more in common with each other than either have with the world of the dog. Most of the difference between us and the dog is due to the fact that our brains work differently.

The greatest difference is in the function of the cortex. This is the part of the brain which is more developed in animals high on the evolutionary scale, being most highly developed in primates. It is not responsible for automatic activities such as breathing or digestion, nor does it have primary control of the experience of emotion. These functions are carried out in lower, more primitive parts of the brain. The cortex is responsible for conscious, deliberate activity and for the more intellectual functions: reason, planning, language, symbolism and memory. It is in these functions that the lower mammals are inferior to dogs and dogs are inferior to people.

This point can be illustrated by comparing one activity, hunting, in all three kinds of mammals. As an example of a primitive mammal, take the hedgehog, which has stayed the same for about fifteen million years. Hedgehogs spend their nights roaming around eating insects and, if they are lucky, food left out for them by conservation-conscious human beings. If this food is put out regularly, a hedgehog is capable of learning where it is likely to be: he will visit the spot regularly. Also, he shows that he prefers human-provided food, such as bread and milk, to his normal diet, by eating it before he eats slugs that are feeding out of the same bowl. But even when he has learnt where this regular food supply is, he does not seem to put the knowledge to good use. Hedgehogs are hard to keep track of, but Pat Morris, a zoologist with a special interest in them, managed to do it by fitting some with harnesses carrying radio transmitters. When he charted the movements of an individual hedgehog, he found that when it started its night-time hunt, it did not necessarily make a bee-line for the food bowl. Sometimes it rambled off in the opposite direction. Sometimes it did not visit the food bowl at all. The result was that some nights, by the time it got there, the food had been eaten by other hedgehogs.

This is very different from a dog's behaviour when

hunting. For one thing, he quickly learns where prey is likely to be found. This can be irritating to owners: a walk in a familiar park often involves visits to all the thickets or trees where he has ever found a squirrel or a rabbit. Also, dogs can profit by experience to improve their hunting strategies: they even learn to co-operate with each other.

Human beings are in quite another league. When Dr Morris hunted hedgehogs, for example, he used a tool: the radio transmitter. He must also have planned ahead: he fitted the transmitter to a hedgehog in advance of the time he wanted to keep track of it. He must also have thought out this course of action without all the elements of the situation being present to his senses: the new combination of a radio transmitter on a hedgehog would be put together and worked out in his mind, before it existed in reality. It is this capacity of the human mind to manipulate concepts or symbols independently of the physical world which sets it apart from that of other animals.

This inability of the dog to think symbolically implies other, more specific differences between dogs and ourselves. For example, dogs cannot understand language. Most people realize this, although at times they pretend otherwise. I overheard an owner in a park one day, expostulating with her dog who was unwilling to leave: 'Now Henry, you know perfectly well that the plumber's coming.' Some owners maintain their dog 'understands every word I say'. This conclusion is usually based on the observation that dogs often seem to respond appropriately when spoken to, wagging their tails if you say 'How about a little trip in the car?' or giving you a sympathetic lick if you say 'I'm really at the end of my tether'. In fact they are responding to your body language and tone of voice. This can be demonstrated by saying something incongruous in the same tone of voice. If you say 'How about some ointment in your ears?' with sufficient enthusiasm you will probably get an enthusiastic response.

Dogs do understand individual words. They can be

trained to obey words of command. They also learn to associate individual words with certain expectations: they may react with excitement when the word 'walk' occurs in a conversation; they usually pay attention when their names are mentioned. But they cannot handle syntax: they cannot understand the combination of words made into new sentences. Although a dog may understand the word 'sit' and the word 'dinner', he would make no sense of the command 'sit in your dinner' if he heard it for the first time.

Although most people will agree with this argument if it is put to them, it is easy to lose sight of its implications and try to communicate with a dog in impossible linguistic ways. As human beings, we can use language to refer to time other than the present, but you cannot discuss the past with a dog or warn him not to do something in the future. It is no use delivering a lecture on obedience to a dog who has run off in the park if you deliver that lecture on his return. He will realize you are angry with him, but he will associate that anger with the action which immediately preceded it: his return. Also, it is no use saying to him 'Don't you dare chew up the tea towels again' before you go out. Better to put them out of the dog's reach.

Another kind of mental activity of which dogs are incapable is understanding the concept of rules. Although rules are part of everyday life for us, to follow a rule or invent a rule actually requires a very sophisticated level of thought. Children only reach that level a few years after they have begun to use language. Until they reach that stage, they cannot, for instance, play the simplest board game, such as snakes and ladders. This is because, even if they can count, they will slide down a ladder or climb a snake if it seems a particularly pretty one.

Dogs operate all the time at a pre-rule level. They can learn to behave in predictable ways, like walking to heel or not touching the food on the table. In the case of specialist, highly trained dogs such as guide dogs, this learned behaviour is so reliable that people can trust their lives to it. But in no instance is this behaviour based on the understanding of a rule or a principle.

This difference has practical implications. It means that it is no use trying to teach a dog something by explaining it to him, even if the explanation takes the form of actions rather than words. To teach a dog something, you have to arrange for him to do the things you require of him, preferably rewarding him afterwards. (This is explained more fully in Chapter 3.) For example, it is no use trying to house-train a dog by drawing his attention to the puddle he has just made on the floor, saying 'No, no', and then taking him outside and showing him where he should have done it. You have to catch him before he urinates and escort him outside so that he urinates there.

This method is, of course, much slower than teaching in terms of rules. It involves the dog in having to repeat the action more often and in a wider range of contexts before you can be satisfied that the behaviour is learnt. Even then, your degree of certainty that the dog will behave as he is supposed to will always be less than if he were capable of learning a rule. If this does not seem obvious, consider the example of a person learning to drive a car round a roundabout. The driving instructor will tell his pupil that on British roads the rule is that he must give way to traffic coming from the right; once he has understood this principle, the pupil will need some practice on real roundabouts, learning how to fit in smoothly with the other traffic. But when he has shown himself competent on one or two roundabouts, he and the instructor will feel fairly satisfied that, armed with the principle he has learnt, he will be able to cope with other roundabouts, even different kinds, such as the little ones without a solid centre. Suppose now, for the sake of argument, that the pupil manages to drive on roundabouts competently, but when the instructor asks him, he can never remember the rule of precedence. Neither the instructor, nor anyone else for that matter, would feel as secure when sitting beside that person.

The inability of dogs to understand rules means that it is wise to err on the side of caution in such matters as keeping a dog on a lead in the street or keeping the gate shut when he is in the garden. He may never have run into the road, but he does not know that he must not do so.

This lack of understanding also means that dogs have no moral sense. They cannot be guilty, they cannot be held responsible, they cannot be blamed. They are also not capable of being activated by such morality-related motives as revenge. Some owners cannot accept this. They will protest that their dog often looks guilty when he has done something 'wrong'. They may say that they know when the dog has messed on the floor in the night, because he slinks away on their arrival in the morning, avoiding their gaze. This 'guilty' look is, however, merely fear. The dog has learnt to associate the presence of a mess on the floor in the morning with the owner's anger.

The fact that dogs are incapable of morality is not just an abstruse philosophical point. Many owners are more upset than they need be by a behavioural lapse on the part of their pet, because they take it personally. They feel that if their dog chews up a precious possession or steals the Sunday joint when their back is turned, he has acted maliciously or inconsiderately. But dogs are not capable of acting from such motives and there is no need to compound the anger inevitably caused by such inconvenience with a sense of personal hurt.

Also, many owners punish their dogs for 'wrong-doing' in order to carry the moral drama through to its proper conclusion. As we shall see in Chapter 3, there are several reasons why punishment is counter-productive as far as the dog is concerned. Owners, on the other hand, often feel frustrated, humiliated even, if they do not punish the dog. It feels much more appropriate to be cleaning up whatever mess the dog has made if he is cowering in a corner having been shouted at or hit, than if he is standing beside you wagging his tail and looking interested. I find that in treating behaviour problems one of the most difficult things is to persuade owners to stop punishing their dogs. But if they realize that the moral drama is entirely in their own minds and makes no sense to the dog, the whole ritual of punishment may seem less attractive.

So much for what dogs cannot do, intellectually. What they can do is not so clear. Up to about fifteen years ago, most studies of animal behaviour started from the assumption that, since you cannot get inside an animal's head and share his thoughts, any explanation of his behaviour must be in terms of things which are observable: the input to his senses (the stimulus) and the output in terms of his behaviour (the response). They discovered that generalizations could be formulated simply in terms of stimulus and response, without reference to any thoughts or feelings in between. These generalizations turned out to be valid and useful. They could be used to predict what an animal would do in a certain set of circumstances. They could also be used to work out methods of teaching animals to do things. As we shall see, for dogs they form the basis of successful obedience training and some kinds of treatment of behavioural problems. But working within the framework of this theory, psychologists tended to slip into the assumption that this was all there was to mental activity in animals: that they always respond automatically, out of habit. Recently, this assumption has been questioned and it has become clear that more goes on in the minds of the higher mammals than robot-like responding to stimuli.

For example, it is clear that the dog's wild ancestor, the wolf, carries in his mind a map of his territory: a wolf will make a journey with an obvious goal (for example, returning to the cubs' den) using a route he has never taken before. There is every reason to think that dogs can do the same. Experiments have shown that dogs are also capable of something called 'delayed response'. You can try with your own dog. One person holds on to him to restrain him, while another person shows him a tit-bit being hidden under one of two cups (Fig. 1). Do not let him go immediately to look for it, but distract him for a while, perhaps even take him into another room. After about twenty minutes bring him back: many dogs will immediately make for the cup with the tit-bit. To guard against the possibility that the dog is guided by smell rather than memory, while he is out of the room you can put a tit-bit under the other cup as well.

Fig. 1 Testing intelligence: show the dog a tit-bit being hidden under one of two cups.

Another puzzle you can give your dog is to set up some kind of fence or barrier between you and him, with a gap or window in it, so that he can see you through it but not reach you. You should arrange it so that the only way he can get to you is by running away from you, round the end of the barrier (Fig. 2). When you call him, most dogs will do just that. Some will not be able to solve the puzzle; young puppies in particular may just sit down and yelp.

Fig. 2 Testing intelligence:
set up a barrier
between you and the dog.

These kinds of intellectual accomplishments may seem trivial to many owners, who take it for granted that their dogs can do this sort of thing and a great deal more. Owners can often tell impressive stories of the clever things their dogs have done. One owner told me about an incident involving her two spaniels, Walter and Wilma, who were on a familiar walk beside a stream. Walter crossed the stream at a shallow part and ran into the wood on the other side. Wilma stayed with her owner but after a few minutes hurried on to a bridge, which was the next point at which Walter could rejoin them. As Wilma waited there expectantly, Walter came running up, not from the expected direction but from behind them on the path: instead of running parallel to them on the other side of the stream, he had retraced his steps and crossed back by the shallow ford. What so impressed this owner, however, was the fact that Wilma's expectation of where he would reappear could not have been based on hearing him or seeing him, but must have been based on memory and inference.

Like all owner's anecdotes, as evidence this has several drawbacks. Firstly, we have to take the owner's word for it: we have no objective record of the event, such as a video recording. And however plausible and trustworthy she may have sounded, psychological experiments have shown that human recall of complex events is unreliable.

Secondly, people tend to impose a retrospective meaning and pattern on a collection of events which may in fact be unconnected. So the owner may have misinterpreted Wilma's behaviour as 'looking for Walter', because she herself was aware that Walter was missing. Wilma might have been looking over the bridge at something completely different, such as another dog. Thirdly, because the exact history of this event is not available, it is hard to know exactly what mental feat Wilma can be credited with performing. How often had Walter crossed the stream and reappeared at the bridge in the past? If he did so on most walks, Wilma had merely learnt that his disappearance at the stream crossing was likely to be followed by his reappearance at the bridge: no reasoning required there. If, on the other hand, Walter had seldom or never run off on this exact route before, Wilma's expectation must have been based on some kind of mental map of the area, coupled with some kind of theorizing about what was going on in Walter's mind: an intellectual feat indeed.

The experimental laboratory situation, although it may seem artificial and arid, has the advantage that it can be reproduced at another time by another person and any findings which it produces can therefore be objectively verified. Until many more laboratory experiments are done, therefore, we cannot make a precise statement about dogs' mental capabilities. All we can say is that they certainly are capable of more than just automatic responding on the basis of habit; they are certainly not capable of mental processes which involve the use of symbols such as language.

Incidentally, there is little doubt that some dogs are more intelligent than others. Some psychologists have argued that there is no such thing as 'intelligence' in dogs, merely various capabilities, such as tracking, herding or guarding. Different dogs, both as breeds and as individuals, may be better at different things; a bloodhound, for example, may be better at tracking than an Afghan, but it does not mean he is more intelligent. This argument misses the point that dogs also possess in varying degrees a more general trait, reflected in the ability to learn quickly and to solve problems like those described earlier. This seems very similar to the kind of trait which in people we call intelligence. It seems reasonable to call it intelligence in dogs, too.

If this chapter has left you with a feeling that you can imagine less well what it is like to be a dog than you could before you read it, then it has succeeded in its object. Although it is difficult to determine precisely a dog's intellectual capabilities, they are undoubtedly so much more limited than those of a human being that they are hard for us to identify with. The best model we have of a dog's thinking processes is that offered to us by learning theory, which is described in the next chapter. Although it certainly does not do justice to a dog's abilities, this theory is useful for predicting what he will do in a given situation. It also helps us to arrange his surroundings so that he will do what we want him to.

3 ● *How Dogs Learn*

For over half a century, hundreds of psychologists all over the world have worked on the problem of how animals learn. Thousands of miles have been run by rats in mazes and millions of words have gone into scientific papers on the subject. Inevitably there have been theoretical disagreements, with feelings running high: psychologists have accused each other of drawing mistaken conclusions from their experiments, even of fudging the statistics or faking the results. What follows is a summary of what appears to have been generally accepted after the dust settled, insofar as it is relevant to dogs.

Animals can learn new behaviour in two ways: via classical conditioning or instrumental learning.

Classical Conditioning

This was first demonstrated by Pavlov, in his famous experiment using dogs. These dogs were strapped into harnesses which limited their movement and fitted with devices which measured the amount of saliva they produced. In the experiment, the dogs heard a bell and immediately afterwards were given food. When this procedure had been repeated a few times, the dogs salivated when the bell was rung, even if no food was produced. To use technical jargon, when the unconditioned stimulus (the food) was paired with the conditioned stimulus (the bell), the conditioned stimulus (the bell) eventually produced the conditioned response (salivation).

This process is called classical conditioning. It occurs in all animals, including human beings, and involves reflex actions, such as the protective eye-blink, and all kinds of other bodily functions not under conscious control. These include heart rate, blood flow, sweating, sleep, digestion and sexual responses. In dogs and man all of these functions can be conditioned to previously irrelevant stimuli. This is why, for example, many people find it harder to get to sleep away from home in strange surroundings: the response of going to sleep has become conditioned to the environment of their own bedroom.

More relevant for dog owners is the fact that bowel and bladder functioning can be conditioned in the same way. A stimulus which instinctively provokes urination in dogs is the smell of old urine: this is why dogs urinate in the same place each time. Other stimuli which are consistently present then become conditioned to the response. If this stimulus is grass or tarmac, the dog is house-trained. If it is the carpet or the duvet, he is not. The task of house-training a puppy consists of arranging that grass or tarmac are paired with urination (and defecation) often enough for conditioning to occur; also, that carpets and duvets are paired with these functions as little as possible: once a connection like this has been learnt it is hard to undo. Unfortunately, in house-training, as with so much in the field of dog behaviour, the depressing moral precept 'prevention is better than cure' applies.

It is important to note here that neither reward nor punishment has any place in classical conditioning. Punishment can actually be counter-productive, as we shall see later in the chapter. Rewards are not necessary either: just the simple pairing of stimulus and response. This means that an owner need not accompany his puppy into a cold, wet garden at 6 am in order to praise his performance. He need only look through the window to make sure it occurs. On the other hand, many owners have to go outside with their puppies anyway, because they will not stay out long enough unless they have company.

The fact that sexual responses can be conditioned is important to some owners. Dogs who have mated with bitches are likely to be more interested in repeating the performance than those who have had no sexual experience. Therefore an owner who does not intend to launch his dog on a serious stud career should not let him try to sire the odd litter to oblige a friend. Breeders who do offer dogs at stud often capitalize on this conditionability to ensure reliable performance. Novice owners bringing their bitches to be mated are often bewildered by the ritual surrounding the mating. A special bit of carpet may be produced for the couple to stand on, the owner of the dog may encourage him verbally and even help him manually in quite intimate ways. This is not done because the dog is too incompetent to manage on his own; it is often partly to prevent the dog from being injured by the bitch, but it is also because the dog's sexual arousal has been conditioned to these particular stimuli. This has the advantage that the dog is more likely to engage in sexual behaviour when it is required and less likely to engage in it when it would be a nuisance, for example, when he is out for a walk.

Some dogs form sexual attachments to a particular object, such as a teddy bear or a rug, grabbing and mounting it whenever they get the chance. Again, this is because his sexual response has become conditioned to this object at some point in his life, probably during adolescence when his sexual behaviour was directed more indiscriminately.

Other emotions can be conditioned too. This is especially true of emotions such as anger or fear which are accompanied by marked physical changes, like increase in heart rate. In this way sights, sounds or smells which are meaningless in themselves can come to arouse powerful feelings in us: by association with some event which moves us deeply. One of the policemen involved in the siege of the Iranian embassy in 1980, when interviewed a year later, said that the smell of the aftershave used by one of the terrorists still made him break out in a sweat of fear.

This kind of thing can also happen to dogs, which is how they can become afraid of the vet's consulting room or get excited by the sight of a lead. Both of these kinds of reaction are discussed more fully in Chapter 5. Dogs can also learn to feel aggressive in certain situations. This is dealt with in Chapter 9.

Once this kind of association has been learned, it can only be unlearned by a process called 'extinction'. Extinction occurs when the conditioned stimulus is no longer paired with the unconditioned stimulus. For example, when, over a series of trials, Pavlov's dogs heard the bell unaccompanied by food, they eventually stopped salivating. This means that behaviour problems which have been caused by faulty conditioning can be cured by extinction. Thus a puppy who has learned to urinate on the sitting-room carpet can be cured by being allowed in the sitting-room under supervision so that the link between being in the sitting-room and urinating can be extinguished. Banishing him from the sitting-room completely will not cure him: if he manages to sneak back into the sitting-room by himself, it is quite likely that he will urinate there again.

In the case of emotions such as fear or excitement, conditioned responses are more difficult to extinguish. The reasons for this and possible ways around the problem are discussed in Chapter 5.

Instrumental Learning

This applies to voluntary actions which result in some kind of reward (as when a rat runs a maze in order to reach the food at the end of it). The basic principle of instrumental learning is that rewarding an action makes its repetition more likely. More specifically, suppose an animal performs an action (or 'response') in a particular situation (or, more technically, in the presence of a certain 'stimulus'), and also suppose that the response is rewarded (or 'reinforced'), then, if the stimulus occurs again, the probability of the animal performing the response is increased. This is the way in which most dogs learn to obey commands. For example, the command 'Sit' (stimulus) is paired with sitting (response) and the dog is praised (reinforcement).

Put like this, the basic principle may seem neither new nor startling, but some of its implications and elaborations are worth a second look. For example, it is important to note that the principle refers merely to the coming together of three events: stimulus, response and reinforcement. It states that whenever three events of this kind occur together, the animal's future behaviour is altered. Therefore when learning to sit, a dog does not need to sit in response to the command 'Sit'. He will learn just as well if he is already in the act of sitting when the owner says 'Sit'. In fact this is the best way to teach a dog to 'obey' a command: wait until he performs the action of his own accord and then say the word of command.

This is comparatively simple in the case of an action such as sitting which dogs perform all the time anyway. Training him to do something he does less frequently, like lying down, can be more of a problem. Many training manuals advocate forcing the dog into the required posture to 'show' him what is required. Some even explain in detail how to compel a dog to lie down when he does not want to, for example by pulling his front legs out from under him, then his back legs, etc. But the aim of training is not to teach a rule of behaviour (remember dogs cannot understand rules) or to explain to the dog what to do, but to arrange for stimulus, response and reinforcement to occur together. It is far more effective, therefore, to reward the dog when he actively takes up the required posture of his own free will than if he is passively forced into it.

It is worth using some ingenuity to arrange this. For example, one way of teaching a dog to lie down is to put a tit-bit on the floor between his front paws, with a cupped hand over it, in such a position that he has to crouch down in order to try to get it. As the dog goes down, the owner says 'Down' and takes away his hand, so that the dog is rewarded with the tit-bit; he is praised at the same time (Fig. 3). When this response is established, the owner still puts his hand on the floor, but now sometimes there is no tit-bit: all the dog gets is praise. Eventually he will go down on command without the hand being placed on the floor at all.

Fig. 3 Teaching without forcing: lying down on command.

Also, in order to learn, a dog does not have to be in a particular 'learning' frame of mind, nor does there have to be a teacher. When the learning is arranged by a teacher, his role is not to convey to the animal a rule of behaviour; it is merely to arrange for stimulus, response and reinforcement to occur in such a way that learning takes place. All this has several implications:

First of all, dogs go on learning even when no one intends to teach them anything. A lot of problem behaviour is a result of this accidental learning. For example, a dog may learn to bark and jump about in the car because this behaviour is 'rewarded' by new and exciting sights appearing at the car window.

Secondly, there is less virtue in training classes than many owners imagine. Owners may think them necessary because they themselves have become accustomed from childhood to the idea that learning occurs in special situations called 'classes'. Admittedly, they can be pleasant social occasions, though for owners of problem dogs they can be a source of embarrassment and dread. If your dog gets a reputation for snapping at other dogs, or even for being a bit restless and spoiling the others' concentration, you may become aware that people are discussing you in the coffee break and manoeuvring to avoid standing next to you in the class. If so, you can stay away with a clear conscience. For the dog, any situation is a potential learning situation: home has much to recommend it.

Thirdly, you cannot teach a dog something simply by dominating him. Just as the British are supposed to try to communicate with foreigners by shouting louder and more fiercely the less they are understood, so they are to be seen in parks bawling like sergeant-majors at dogs who are refusing to 'stay' or 'come'. But the successful trainer of a dog is neither dominating nor overbearing, but an unobtrusive stage-manager, arranging for the appropriate stimuli and rewards to occur at the right time. If a dog does not appear to be learning what is intended, it is no use getting angry. What is needed is cool detachment, in order to puzzle out what is going wrong.

There are other aspects of instrumental learning which are relevant for owners:

Rewards

Rewards are essential to instrumental learning. The rewards which conventional dog trainers most often use are praise and petting. They sometimes use tit-bits, although these are often viewed as undesirable and corrupting, somehow smacking of bribery. Praise is certainly convenient: it can be given at once, it does not need any equipment and you can do it from a distance. It does not have a moral advantage over any other reward, however. Sometimes a delicious piece of cheese has much greater incentive value and, if so, it is silly not to use it. Also, in a dog's life there is usually a wide range of experiences which he finds rewarding: for example, going out into the garden, having a ball thrown, meeting another dog. These can all be used when you are trying to change your dog's behaviour.

The reward value of all kinds of happenings in a dog's life can also help to explain a lot of problem behaviour. Often there is a hidden reward which keeps the behaviour going.

> Miss Hamilton consulted me about her Norfolk terrier, Harry, because of his behaviour on car journeys. He barked and jumped about so much when the car was going that she could not concentrate on the driving. The barking started as soon as she turned on the ignition. It was worse on certain routes, such as the journey to the local park. Trips into town were better. She had tried shouting at him, but that did no good. She sometimes gave him a smack with a free hand when she could reach him, but that did no good either.

Harry's behaviour might seem crazy, but it makes sense when viewed as being rewarded by what followed. Harry had learnt that a ride to the park was always followed by an enjoyable walk. As he barked, the car got nearer the park and the walk: these experiences rewarded the barking. Miss Hamilton's attention was no doubt rewarding to him too. Most dogs are very sociable beings, for whom social interaction is highly attractive. They crave it so much that the interaction does not even have to be friendly. As with children sometimes, they prefer angry attention to no attention.

The Johnstone family consisted of mother, grandmother, three children and a little mongrel, Jimmy. They all talked at once, while Jimmy weaved in and out of their legs, snuffling and pawing at them. Sometimes he broke off to make social overtures to me or to bark at a noise outside the door. The Johnstones yelled and swatted at him continually. At the same time they tried to tell me how he was 'off his trolley': always on the go, always pestering them. When he heard any noise outside, like the ice-cream chimes, he barked and barked and would not stop. When letters came through the door, it was a race to get there before he chewed them up.

It was likely that there were several factors operating to produce Jimmy's hyperactive state. One was probably his basic temperament, genetically determined. However, there was also little doubt that it was kept going by rewards like being chased and shouted at. I asked the Johnstones what they did when Jimmy was quiet. Not surprisingly, they replied that they took these opportunities to get on with their lives; they took no notice of him when he was resting in his basket: so Jimmy was not rewarded at all for being good.

Timing of rewards

With rewards, timing is crucial. They must be delivered at the same time as the response to be learnt or immediately afterwards. A delay of even one second can weaken the effect. So there is no point in giving a dog a chocolate drop at the end of a training session, 'because he has been such a good boy'.

It would seem at first sight that the nicer a reward is and the greater the incentive it provides, the more effective it will be. But experiments have shown that the matter is more complicated. If an animal is too highly motivated, this can actually disrupt his performance. In fact the optimum level of motivation decreases as the complexity of the task increases. This generalization is known as the Yerkes-Dodson law. So, in an emergency while driving the car, terror will make us apply the brake quickly and effectively, but fright in an exam can stop our brains functioning. Applied to learning in dogs, the Yerkes-Dodson law means that when an owner is trying to train a simple response, such as coming when called, he should use an extremely attractive reward, such as a delicious tit-bit. On the other hand, when the response is more complex or calls for calmness and self-control (for example sitting still when visitors arrive), a very attractive reward may have a counter-productive effect: it may increase the dog's excitement. It may be better to praise the dog mildly.

Extinction

Extinction is the technical term for what happens when a response is unlearned. If a learned response is never rewarded it will eventually be extinguished and disappear. In fact, making sure that a response is never rewarded is the safest, most reliable way of eliminating it from an animal's repertoire. An owner who wants to stop a dog begging for food should ignore it, rather than shouting at it or smacking it. The dog will eventually stop. Extinction may take some time to work. In fact, when a response which has previously been rewarded is suddenly not rewarded any more, to begin with that response is performed more often, before its frequency starts to decline. A dog who has been used to getting tit-bits when he begs at table will not give up as soon as his owners decide not to give him any more. He will whine and paw their knees more frantically for a while before he finally accepts the new regime.

Extinction was the principle used in the treatment of Miss Hamilton's dog Harry, who barked in the car. The barking was being encouraged by all kinds of rewards, particularly by the car approaching exciting destinations

and by Miss Hamilton's attention. The aim was to withdraw all these rewards. Whenever Harry started to bark,
Miss Hamilton was instructed to ignore him and to pull
into the side of the road. When he had quietened down,
she was to move off again. This was a tiresome regime,
involving many car trips which were simply training trips
with no certainty of reaching a destination. Also, Miss
Hamilton was discouraged because, to begin with, Harry's
bark became more penetrating and his shuttling to and fro
in the car more frantic. She persisted, however, and after
a few weeks he improved.

Schedules of reinforcement

The speed and permanence of learning are affected by
what is technically known as the schedule of reinforcement: whether an animal is rewarded every time he performs a response, is rewarded for every ten responses
or whether the reward arrives randomly, and so on. It
was found that the quickest learning takes place on a
one hundred per cent reinforcement schedule, i.e. when
the response is rewarded every time it happens. On the
other hand, once a response has been learnt, a variable
interval schedule makes it more resistant to extinction: if
the response is only rewarded every so often, unpredict-
ably, it is less likely to be unlearned. Some psychologists
think that this is why activities such as gambling, which
are randomly rewarded, can become so addictive.

Therefore, when you are teaching a dog to sit, for
example, to begin with you should reward him every time
he gets it right. Once he is sitting reliably on command,
you should gradually reduce the frequency of the reward:
first of all reward every other correct response, then every
third one and so on. It is particularly important to do this
with responses which would eventually become extremely
inconvenient or impossible to reward all the time. For
example, every time you tell him to go to his basket, you
do not want to have to run over to him with a tit-bit.

A great deal of problem behaviour is kept going by variable interval reinforcement. This means it is hard to cure. The dog who pesters and whines for attention probably does not get attention all the time, but only now and again, depending on the mood of the owners and on how busy they are. This does not mean that the response will never be extinguished, but that it takes longer.

Stimulus generalization
When a response has been learned to a particular stimulus, it is likely to be performed in the presence of similar stimuli as well. So, if a dog develops a fear of thunder, he may eventually start to show fear at the sound of any loud noise. In the same way, a dog who has developed the habit of barking when the bell rings, because he has learned to associate this sound with the arrival of visitors, may start to bark at other similar sounds, such as the telephone ringing or even ice-cream van chimes.

Shaping
This is a method of teaching complicated responses (like opening a door by pressing on the handle) which the dog would be unlikely to perform spontaneously if left to himself. It is how animal trainers get their animals to do all kinds of unlikely things such as jumping through burning hoops or riding bicycles. It involves rewarding the dog whenever he makes the best try of which he is capable at what you want him to do. To teach your dog by this method to open the door, you might start by rewarding him for going to the door on command; then he would not be rewarded until he put his paws on the door; then he would have to put his paws higher and higher on the door before he got a reward; after that he would only be rewarded when he put his paws on the door handle, then when he pressed down on the handle; finally he would be rewarded only when he pressed the handle so that the door opened.

Most people do not want to teach their dog to open doors: in fact they would prefer it if he could not. But there are 'tricks' which are more useful, if less spectacular. One of these is the ability to sit quietly in a designated place (e.g. in a dog basket) on command. To the owner of an excitable dog this may seem an impossible pipe-dream. But it is wonderful what shaping can do. First of all, you reward the dog for going to his basket, then for staying there with you beside him. After that he has to wait for his reward for gradually increasing lengths of time, with you still beside him. The next step might be for you gradually to move increasing distances away from him, always coming back to reward him. Finally he only gets a reward after you have been out of sight and then returned. Note that during this process you should always reward the dog in his basket. Never call him to you for a reward, because then you would be rewarding something you do not want him to do: running up to you, rather than staying put.

Punishment
Punishment is the most over-used technique in dog training. For many owners, it is the method they first use to stop undesirable behaviour. It should be a last resort.

People often assume that punishment has the opposite effect to reward: that, if paired with a response, it tends to reduce the probability of that response in the future. This is not so. The opposite of reward is absence of reward; if a response is not rewarded, it will eventually be extinguished. Punishment has more complex and unpredictable effects, which are not always the ones intended.

Experiments have shown that if a moderate level of punishment is used (which is the only kind most sane owners would be prepared to use), the animal may stop the punished activity, but only temporarily. He will eventually start up the behaviour again. The only kind of punishment which dissuades an animal from doing something permanently is an experience of traumatic severity. In 1953, two American psychologists, Solomon and Wynne, did an experiment in which dogs were put into a pen with an electrified floor; a buzzer sounded, then a shock was turned on. The only means of escape was to jump out of the pen, which most dogs did. However, the shock was so severe that some dogs died. Those who survived were put back in the pen and the buzzer sounded again. Although they were never shocked again, they always jumped, even after hundreds of trials. If therefore you want to be sure of dissuading your dog from doing something by punishment, you must be prepared to do something very nasty to him, which gives him a terrible fright. This could only possibly be justified as a last resort. One extreme measure, the shock collar, will be discussed later in the chapter.

In addition to being ineffective, punishment may have undesirable side-effects. It may increase the dog's general level of stress, for example. If the dog is placid and his owner shouts at him or hits him only rarely, this effect is not likely to be significant. But if the dog is anxious, excitable or has behaviour problems which are caused by stress in the first place, a vicious circle may be set up: the more the dog is punished the more upset he gets and the more upset he gets the worse he behaves.

Another, more specific form of stress which can be caused by punishment is conflicting feelings about the owner. Once a dog has become attached to his owner, it is very difficult to break that attachment. If the owner behaves in a cruel or frightening way, the dog's fear of him will co-exist with the attachment, putting him in all kinds of dilemmas. It is fairly easy to empathize with this predicament, as there are plenty of parallels in human experience. Perhaps one of the most agonizing is the situation of children who are abused by their parents: these parents are often the only love objects they have and, in spite of the abuse, they are often very distressed when they are separated from them. There are plenty of experimental parallels too. Suppose, for example, a rat is taught to run along a passage to get food, then he is given an electric shock as he eats. The result is that he will run eagerly some way along the passage until he gets near the food bowl, then he will stop and appear to be stuck: unable to go on or to go back. He may also show some more dramatic signs of stress, such as having a fit.

Some punishments have the opposite effect to that intended because they act as rewards at the same time; the two are not mutually exclusive. This is most likely to apply to a punishment which involves a social interaction with the owner, for, as has been mentioned earlier, a dog is such a social being that sometimes being taken notice of, even to be punished, is preferable to being ignored.

Mrs Boyd consulted me about her Alsatian, Buddy, who was hard to control in various ways. One example was his behaviour when she picked up his lead to take him out for a walk. She demonstrated this to me in the consulting room by taking a lead out of her pocket: immediately Buddy, who had been lying quietly, jumped up, grabbed it and started dashing and leaping at Mrs Boyd, shaking the lead like a rat. I asked her to show me how she tried to stop him. She swatted at him ineffectually with her hands and said 'No, Buddy, no' in a pleading voice. This only seemed to provoke a fresh bout of leaping and shaking.

Because dogs cannot understand language, it is not possible to be sure that the dog knows what he is being punished for: sometimes a misunderstanding arises which leads to further problems.

Mr Ross was a small man. He wore a sweat shirt which proclaimed his membership of a martial arts club. He had three Alsatians, two of whom he had trained to be 'good watch dogs': they growled on command. The third,

Rambo, he despaired of, however. Rambo had never shown any aggression to anyone. Furthermore, the last straw, he was not, and never had been, house-trained. When I inquired into the details of this, it became clear why: Rambo had been trapped since puppyhood in a vicious circle with Mr Ross. Whenever Mr Ross came upon Rambo in the act of urinating or defecating in the house, he would hit and shout at him. Rambo would cower in fear. Mr Ross would then rush Rambo outside and they would spend a fruitless half hour, with Rambo standing around looking uneasy and Mr Ross exhorting him to get on with it. Eventually they would come inside again. Rambo would creep away into another room away from Mr Ross and urinate or defecate there.

What was happening was this: Rambo learned to associate punishment with urinating or defecating in Mr Ross's presence. So when Mr Ross went outside with him, he did not perform there, because he expected punishment. The only course open to him was to wait until he could get away from Mr Ross, which was when he came inside again.

Unlearning bad behaviour: alternatives to punishment
If punishment is too risky, how can bad behaviour be corrected? The most reliable way of stopping a dog from doing something you do not want him to do is to arrange that the behaviour is extinguished, i.e. that it is not rewarded. An example of extinction in action was seen in the case of Harry, who barked in the car. His owner cured this by making sure that the barking was not followed by anything pleasurable.

Extinction has the disadvantage that it takes time. It usually needs many repetitions of the undesirable behaviour before it takes effect and in some cases what the dog is doing may be so undesirable that the owner cannot allow him to do it again and again. One example of this might be the dog who picks up things around the house, runs off with them and chews them. Often this behaviour is rewarded by the excitement and perturbation which it produces. A woman once brought me her dog complaining that he dug up worms in the garden, brought them indoors and ate them in her sight. This disgusted her so much that she always jumped up and tried to stop him: he just picked them up in his mouth and ran off to the bedroom to eat them, which was worse. I advised her to pay no attention to him, as I was pretty sure that her attention was acting as a reward. Unfortunately my theory was not tested out in this instance, because she could not bear to act on it. In fact she was quite indignant, as if I had suggested she condone some really immoral behaviour.

Most people might be able to ignore this particular behaviour, but there are other kinds of stealing-and-chewing which no one can ignore. Another dog, a springer spaniel, was brought to me because he stole bits of paper and ripped them up. The trouble was that he seemed to be able to tell (presumably by close observation of the owner's behaviour) which were important documents, liable to provoke gratifying excitement when stolen. (I took it as a compliment when, after our consultation, the owner telephoned me to ask for another copy of the letter I sent them summarizing my advice: the dog had chewed it up.)

In all such cases the owner has to intervene and do something to the dog to stop the behaviour. It is not appropriate to call this intervention punishment, because this implies that the intervention must be upsetting to the dog and must convey a moral message to him. To be successful, the intervention has to work in one of three ways. Firstly, it could distract the dog from what he is doing. A puppy who is just about to squat on the carpet to urinate might be distracted by calling his name; for an older dog who is rushing to the window to bark at the postman, a blast from an anti-mugging alarm might be enough to catch his attention. Secondly, it could physically prevent the dog from performing the response, by for example holding his jaws shut when he starts barking. Finally, an intervention might neutralize the rewarding effects of the response by a counter-balancing unpleasant experience. An example of this is curing a dog of stealing food by booby-trapping it with mustard or peppers. It is important to note that in none of these cases need the intervention be so unpleasant that the dog is seriously upset.

To be most effective, the intervention should be made as early in the sequence of undesirable behaviour as possible. Once a dog is caught up in the excitement of some forbidden activity, whether it be barking at the postman or chasing cars, it is often impossible to stop him, except by extreme means. On the other hand, a sharp word or startling sound just as the dog notices the interesting stimulus and is gathering himself to respond may be enough to stop it. By now it should be clear that an intervention made even a short time *after* the response is completely ineffective. There is no point in smacking a dog when you find a puddle on the carpet or a chewed dishcloth; the dog simply cannot make any sense of that event.

One problem about intervening to stop undesirable behaviour is that some behaviour occurs only when the owner is not there or is too far away to be able to stop it. Common problems of this kind are dogs who raid the refrigerator while the owners are out of the room or who chase cats in the garden. In these cases, a booby-trap can be useful. Electrically sophisticated people are at an advantage here, as battery-operated burglar alarms wired up to the no-go areas can be effective.

In fact these 'Acts of God' interventions have additional advantages over those which are not obviously connected with the owner. They run no risk of arousing fear of the owner. Also, they do not lead to the dog learning that it is safe to do the forbidden thing as long as the owner is not present. For these reasons, it is sometimes a good idea to use 'remote' interventions, even when you are present. Something soft, like a cushion, thrown at the dog; a light, noisy object, like a can with pebbles in it, thrown near him; a pocket anti-mugging alarm set off by the owner – these can all seem like Acts of God to the dog, at least for a time. The effect may be limited because the startling effect of these happenings may wear off. Also, many dogs seem to realize eventually that the owner is responsible for them.

Whatever the intervention consists of, immediately the dog has stopped doing the undesirable thing, the owner should provide and encourage the dog to do something else and then reward it: he needs to be taught what he should do, not merely what he should not do. For example, an owner who sees his dog going to investigate a bit of rubbish on a walk, might stop him by calling out 'No' sharply; then he might immediately call the dog to him and reward him with a tit-bit for coming.

To illustrate some of these points, here are two examples: in one situation the owner uses punishment wrongly; in the other, he uses it correctly.

Example 1: An owner comes home to find that his dog has disembowelled and chewed up a cushion. *It is likely that this behaviour is provoked by stress in the first place: any form of punishment should be avoided.* He shouts 'Bad dog, look what you've done'. *The punishment is too late for the dog to make any connection between it and the bad behaviour.* The dog cowers down. The owner smacks him until he yelps. *There is hardly ever any need to make a dog that upset.* He finally escapes, lies down in his basket and is subdued for the rest of the afternoon. *Don't be fooled. The dog may seem to be 'sorry' or 'on his best behaviour'. He is probably just keeping away from the owner out of fear. There is a high probability that later he will need to chew up another cushion to calm his nerves.*

Example 2: A lively young golden retriever develops the habit of jumping up on his owner when he greets him. This is becoming a nuisance, so every time he jumps up, the owner ignores him as far as possible. *The reward of attention from the owner is removed.* He also steps gently on one of the dog's hind feet, until he loses his balance and puts all four feet on the ground. *The intervention is made as the response is being performed. It is only forceful enough to stop the response, not forceful enough to cause distress. It does not obviously come from the owner; the dog begins to form the impression that if he jumps up he will overbalance.* As the dog goes down, the owner says 'Sit' and praises him. *Once the undesirable response has stopped, the dog is rewarded for performing a desirable response, namely greeting the owner with all four feet on the ground.*

Shock collars

These devices can be bought in the USA but their sale is banned in Great Britain. A battery is incorporated in the collar, which has two studs on its inside that make contact with the dog's skin. The shock is delivered via these studs. Some collars work on the same principle as a radio-controlled toy car or aeroplane, with a transmitter sending instructions at long range to deliver the shock; these are used to deliver punishment in situations where the owner is too far away from the dog to be able to influence him. Others incorporate a noise sensor in the collar itself, so that every time the dog barks he gets a shock. They are used to tackle the problem of the dog which barks incessantly when the owner is out.

The first reaction of many dog-lovers is that the collars are inhumane, which is why their sale is banned in Great Britain. Certainly, the anti-barking collars can inflict pro-longed suffering on a dog, because they do not always work as they are meant to. Sometimes they can be activated by noises other than the dog's own bark, so the dog may be exposed to shocks he cannot learn to avoid: a very efficient way of increasing his stress level. Also, it is possible for a vicious circle to be set up, whereby the dog yelps when he gets a shock, the yelp activates the shock again and so on.

The radio-activated shock collars are not subject to these drawbacks and it is said that they have been used successfully to cure dogs of habits such as sheep-chasing, although I have never personally been involved in such a case. The dog is apparently given the shock when he has seen the sheep and is running towards them. A few trials are said to be enough to deter him. From a theoretical point of view, however, the shock would have to be a traumatic one in order to deter the dog permanently after one or two trials. It is possible under laboratory conditions to deliver a shock level which is unpleasant but not dangerous. To do it by remote control to a dog who is on the move would be a procedure subject to much more error. In my view, using the collar in such a way could only be justified if the dog were in danger of being destroyed if he did not mend his ways. This could well be the case with sheep-chasing, but in most other situations (like jogger-chasing or car-chasing) it is better to look for another way of solving the problem (see Chapter 9).

4 • *Instinctive Behaviour*

Dogs do a great number of things by instinct, more things than we do. As you go up the evolutionary ladder, the proportion of activities in which learning plays a part increases. A bitch can usually look after her litter of puppies adequately, even if it is her first; human mothers are at sea without friends, relatives or baby books to help them. Female chimpanzees need to be shown how to breast-feed their babies.

Instinctive patterns of behaviour are inherited, along with physical characteristics such as coat colour or shape of head, although some may not show themselves until the dog is grown up. Instinctive behaviour to do with mothering will be dealt with in Chapter 5 and that to do with urination and defecation in Chapter 11. Here, what will be looked at is dog's instinctive social behaviour.

Because dogs are sociable animals like ourselves and because they obviously form genuine loving relationships with us, it is easy to fall into the trap of assuming that, in these relationships, they follow the same social conventions as us. This assumption can lead to misunderstandings and shocks for the owner because dogs' social conventions (which in their case are inherited) are in fact rather different.

> Mr Watson, the owner of William, an elderly cairn terrier, was watching television one evening, with William as usual sitting on Mr Watson's knee. The programme was about the benefits of pet-keeping: some research was being described which showed that keeping a pet

reduced your chances of having a heart attack. Mr Watson affectionately patted and fondled William, saying 'You're my anti-heart attack medicine'. William promptly bit Mr Watson.

As will be seen later in the chapter, William had not gone off his head or turned savage but was behaving completely in character; and if Mr Watson had been able to read the social cues that William was giving, he would not have had the fright he did.

People who have grown up with dogs and are accustomed to handling them are often scornful of inexperienced owners who cannot control their dogs. They feel these ineffectual owners must suffer from some weakness of character. What they do not realize is that people have to learn to understand a dog's communications; many 'doggy' people acquire this skill so early that they feel the knowledge is instinctive: it is not. People often compare owning a puppy to having a child. There are similarities, of course: both are dependent creatures, with round-the-clock physical and emotional needs. But there is an important difference.

This was brought forcibly home to me when, at the same time as seeing problem dogs, I ran evening classes in 'Psychology for Mothers'. I had planned a series of group discussions in which the mothers would feel free to express and explore their feelings, but I discovered that the mothers themselves wanted something different. Although they would ask me such questions as whether they should pick up their babies when they cried or whether it was time to potty-train their toddlers, it became more and more apparent that these mothers were not suffering from lack of knowledge; most mothers do not have to be told these things by a stranger. They are the people who know their own children best and are in a better position than anyone else to know when is the right time to pick them up or bring a potty to them.

Babies are born with an instinctive repertoire of social

behaviour which fits in exactly with that of their mothers. For instance, babies respond more eagerly to a human face which moves and talks than to one which is motionless; and more to a human voice which changes in pitch than to a monotone. For their part, mothers (and other human beings) when talking to babies automatically exaggerate their facial expressions and talk in a special 'baby' voice, with marked modulations in pitch. This automatic reaction is probably partly instinctive and partly learned: after all we were all babies once and we must know (even if we are not conscious of it) what babies like. In the same way, mothers instinctively respond to a cry of distress from their babies. They also very soon learn to tell the difference between that kind of cry and the kind of cry which does not need such immediate attention. The mothers who came to the classes were not in need of factual information, although they thought they were. What they needed was more self-confidence: they needed to be less anxious, so that they could follow their own instincts and trust their own judgement.

Novice dog-owners, on the other hand, are often simply in need of information. They do not have a repertoire of instinctive responses designed to mesh with that of the dogs. Nor have they intuitive knowledge of what it is like to be a dog, never having been dogs. Most new owners manage by trial and error, working on the assumption that dogs are small furry people. This enables most dogs and owners to rub along most of the time, but, because the fundamental assumption is faulty, it is common for things to go awry, as they did for Mr Watson. To find out the rules governing dog social behaviour we must turn to scientific observation.

To study most kinds of instinctive behaviour in animals, it is usually enough to observe the animals themselves. But with social behaviour in dogs this undertaking is complicated by the fact that most dogs are heavily involved with human beings. Observing human–dog interaction is often like listening to a 'Is this Wembley, no it's Thursday' kind of conversation, where neither side completely understands the other. In addition, even where human beings are not directly involved in the process of selective breeding, domestication has resulted in the distortion of some inherited, instinctive patterns of behaviour, with the result that it may be hard to appreciate their significance. For example, when weaning their puppies, it is natural for bitches to regurgitate food for them: a form of liquidized baby food. But domestic dogs often do this in a disorganized way, vomiting when the puppies are not there; or they may eat the regurgitated food themselves. Owners are often understandably mystified by this.

Other aspects of the behaviour of some breeds may be hard to interpret because they are parts of a puppy's repertoire which selective breeding has caused to be carried on into adult life, a phenomenon known as neoteny. One example is friendliness towards strangers. In wild dogs this behaviour is shown only by puppies. Its function seems to be protection against attack: since puppies cannot hope to win in a fight with a strange hostile dog, their best chance is to appease it. Many domestic dogs continue this indiscriminate friendliness as adults. In its extreme form, this can be disconcerting: instead of attacking burglars, they seem delighted at their arrival. But in a more moderate form, it has obvious advantages.

The best way to learn about dogs' social behaviour is to study their wild ancestor, the wolf. It used to be thought that because the appearance of different breeds of dog varies so enormously, they could not all be descended from the same species. Wolves and jackals were thought to be the most likely candidates. But it now seems likely that, in spite of apparent differences in appearance, the basic anatomy of all dogs is so similar to that of the wolf that all other canine species can be ruled out as ancestors.

Archaeological evidence suggests that the wolf was first domesticated about ten thousand years ago, in the Near

East. It is common for those who do not see the appeal of pet-keeping to regard it as a luxury, only indulged in by modern Western societies with more money than sense. However, it is, on the contrary, a universal human activity. Primitive tribes in South America, for example, keep small mammals and birds; sometimes they even breast-feed the mammals themselves. So it is plausible to suppose that Near Eastern tribes ten thousand years ago hand-reared wolf cubs and kept them as pets. They would have discovered that tame wolves were useful as well as appealing. They could help with hunting and they could act as watch-dogs.

One of the major differences between the temperament of wolves and dogs is that wolves are, on the whole, much less docile. They are both more fearful and more aggressive. Once hand-reared wolves started to breed with each other, the less tame ones were probably allowed to go back to the wild. This would be the beginning of selective breeding and of domestication. As we have seen, in this process of domestication, instinctive behaviour patterns, as well as physical appearance, have been altered. Some which are not necessary for survival in a domestic environment have become fragmented and disorganized. Others which are convenient in a domestic animal have become exaggerated. An example of this is sexual behaviour. Wolves are not sexually mature until they are about two years old, whereas dogs mature at half that age. Also female wolves come into season only once a year, half as often as most bitches. To most owners nowadays, this may seem a positive advantage; but for the purposes of selective breeding the quicker the generations follow each other the better. In addition, many breeds have special abilities and personality characteristics which are typical of the breed. Greyhounds track a prey by sight, pointers by smell; Dobermanns have a strong guarding instinct, and so on. All these behaviour patterns, such as guarding, pointing and tracking, can be seen in the wolf. Selective breeding has exaggerated and refined these characteristics, but it has not produced them.

Studying wild wolves presents a problem, however, because they are hard to observe at close quarters. They are timid, they have an acute sense of smell and they move around a lot. On the other hand, if they are kept as pets, their behaviour becomes distorted, like that of dogs. The best solution seems to be for an observer to aim to act rather like an anthropologist doing field work: to be accepted enough by them to be able to observe them, but to take care to interfere minimally with their lives. A zoologist, Eric Zimen, working in Bavaria, managed this solution by hand-rearing a few wolf cubs and keeping them in a large enclosure. When the second generation was born, he made their acquaintance as cubs and was accepted by them. His findings by and large confirmed those of previous workers, but his close contact meant that he could fill in the fine detail. One of the main conclusions to be drawn is that the goings-on between wolves are extremely subtle and complex: there is still a great deal more to be learned. For example, it seems that they are capable of multi-layered social manoeuvres such as pretending or bluffing. In order to get something he wants, like a bone, a wolf may entice the others away with an invitation to play, then rush in and grab it.

A wolf pack consists of an extended family group of both sexes: grandparents, aunts, cousins and so on. A wolf will live all his life in this pack, unless he breaks away to form a new one. The pack spends most of its time together: hunting, feeding, sleeping and playing. Mating takes place between pack members, and all pack members help with the upbringing of the cubs.

In efficient human organizations, which depend on team work, some time is usually devoted to cementing social bonds. In happy schools, for example, there are often end-of-term parties for the staff. In the same way, in wolf packs there are regular activities whose only purpose seems to be to reinforce social cohesion. Morning and evening, pack members greet each other muzzle-to-muzzle; In the evenings, there might also be a howling session: a kind of community sing-song.

Another kind of greeting is anal/genital sniffing, the kind of thing dogs do a great deal when they meet in the park. Wolves do it much less than muzzle-to-muzzle greeting, seemingly because it is not so necessary when there is constant contact with each other. These anal and genital smells convey a great deal of information: certainly information to do with gender and sexual readiness, and probably much more. This sniffing seems more like the kind of conversation which people have when they meet at a party: an interchange designed to find out where the other person fits into the scheme of things. The muzzle-to-muzzle greeting seems a more casual, friendly exchange.

Dominance

In a wolf pack, the social structure always takes the form of a dominance hierarchy, with a leader, a second-in-command and so on. In fact, there are two hierarchies, one for each sex. A wolf's place in the hierarchy influences every aspect of his life; he is acutely aware all the time of where he stands. We all know people like this, who are so rivalrous that they view every social interchange from a competitive angle; in conversation they always have to show they know more, work harder or have cleverer children. People who behave in that way are irritating because their preoccupation seems unnecessary, arising perhaps out of some insecurity. For wolves, however, their survival depends on this hierarchy. They can only tackle large prey, such as caribou, if they hunt in a well-organized pack. Also, the pack can only look after a limited number of cubs each year: not every bitch can be allowed a litter.

In practice, only the top male and female wolf mate with each other. Other lower-rank wolves may form temporary alliances with the leaders, but these are broken up by the higher-rank partner. A lower-rank female wolf may show interest in the top male, for example; but the top female soon steps in and sees her off. Female wolves at the bottom of the hierarchy may not even come into season. Dominant wolves tend to be older and larger than the subordinate ones, but dominance also depends on force of personality. The consequence is that if you are a wolf, in order to breed you have to be ambitious. As this personality characteristic seems, at least to some extent, to be inherited, this type is therefore preserved down the generations.

Dogs also have this awareness of their position in the dominance hierarchy. For them, the pack consists of the family they live in, including both human and other canine members. In their case, however, the survival of the species does not depend on this awareness and so, as with other behavioural characteristics, the strength of the preoccupation varies in different breeds and from one individual to another. Some dogs are constantly on the look-out for a chance to seize the dominant role in a household. Others do not seem to be concerned with the issue at all. Male dogs and those from guarding or fighting breeds (Alsatians, Dobermanns, the various Scottish terriers) are more likely to be obsessed with dominance. Those which are bred as companion dogs or gun dogs (spaniels, Labradors) are less so. This lowered awareness of dominance in some dogs may be another example of neoteny; young wolves do not have a clear dominance hierarchy either: such preoccupations only come with adulthood.

How can you tell what position a dog or a wolf holds in the dominance hierarchy? The most obvious expression of dominance is his body language. If a dog or wolf draws himself up to his full height, with his ears up, the hair on the back of his neck raised and his tail up, looking the other pack member straight in the eye (Fig. 4), he is saying: 'I'm dominant over you and you had better back down.' Darwin was the first scientist to see the significance of this dominant posture. He pointed out that all its features were designed to make the dog appear as tall as possible.

Fig. 4 A typical dominant posture.

If the dog growls as well, or bares his teeth, not many people would mistake his message. Without these clues, however, it is possible to overlook it. This is particularly true of the long-haired, flop-eared breeds, where it can be hard to make out what is going on underneath. There are other dominant postures, too, which are even easier to misinterpret. For example, which of the two dogs in Fig. 5 is dominant? In fact it is the dog on the right, who is giving the left-hand dog the message 'You have pushed me far enough. If you don't stop pestering me, I will attack you.'

Another common dominant posture is shown in Fig. 6,

Fig. 5 Which dog is dominant?

Fig. 6 Puppies practising behaviour patterns: dominance.

where the dominant puppy is standing over the other. Puppies do this 'standing over' with one another in their play, alternately taking up the dominant role. It often happens in a more disguised form between dogs and their owners. If a dog is preoccupied with dominance, he may express this dominance by putting his paws on his owner's shoulders or on her lap or even by sitting in her lap. Owners often unwittingly express dominance over their dogs by standing over them and reaching down to pat them. It is in this kind of situation that surprise attacks by the dog often happen. This is probably what happened in the case of Mr Watson and William. William considered himself to be dominant over Mr Watson. He expressed this by sitting on Mr Watson's knee. When Mr Watson cuddled him, William interpreted this as a dominance challenge and promptly retaliated.

If a dog or wolf takes up one of these dominant postures, unless the other individual signals his submission, the dominant one will attack. There are two obvious submissive body postures. In 'active submission' (Fig. 7) the dog crouches down, gaze averted, ears back and tail lowered. Darwin pointed out that in this posture the dog was making himself as short as possible. In 'passive submission' (Fig. 8), the dog rolls on his side with one back leg in the air. He may even urinate.

But even without these explicit body postures, dogs and wolves are all the time signalling their relative status to one another. It has been found that in species such as hens or rhesus monkeys, which live in hierarchies, there is a constant difference between the behaviour of subordinate and dominant animals. High-ranking animals tend to start the most social initiatives and respond to the fewest: the position is reversed for subordinate animals. In the case of wolves, the leader starts most new activities, such as hunting, howling, resting, etc. If a subordinate approaches him, for instance to greet him, he tends to ignore the subordinate. Ignoring is very dominant behaviour, a fact

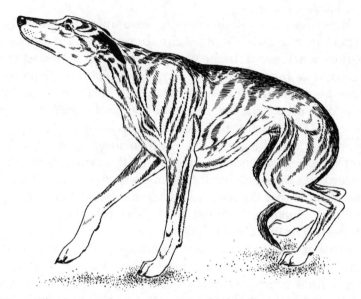

Fig. 7 Active submission.

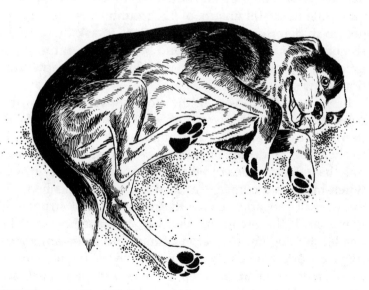

Fig. 8 Passive submission.

which can be put to practical use with dogs, as we shall see later.

How does a wolf or a dog gain dominance over the others in his pack? Wolves do sometimes fight pitched battles to achieve it. In the pack which Zimen observed the outcome of these fights was sometimes fatal, but this may have been because the wolves were kept in an enclosure: it was difficult for the loser to leave the pack completely, as he could in the wild. But household dogs are like Zimen's wolves in that they, too, live in an enclosed space. If dogs in the same household start fighting, their owners should regard this as a potentially serious situation: they should not assume that the dogs will settle matters between them without bloodshed. (What to do about fighting dogs is discussed more fully in Chapter 9.)

Most of the time, however, dominance issues are raised and worked out in a much more subtle way. A wolf or a dog with upwardly mobile ambitions might start his climb on the ladder by challenging those close to him in rank. He may do so by taking up an overtly dominant body posture, but while he is still unsure of his ground he is more likely just to initiate some social interaction, to ask them to do something. If the others respond or give way, rather than ignoring him, he will assume that they have accepted his dominant status.

In the case of wolves, all the wolves involved know the conventions and are aware of what is happening. With domestic dogs, on the other hand, most of their pack is likely to be made up of human beings who at best will only have a hazy idea of what is going on. If a dog growls when his owner comes near his food bowl or his bed, his owner will probably realize that some kind of struggle is going on. If the owner backs away, he usually knows he has let the dog get the better of him. But some ambitious dogs test out their dominance merely by asking for things. They may come up to their owners and paw them for attention, bark at the door to be let out or bring a ball to be thrown. Every time the owner obliges, these dogs take this as another bit of evidence that they are dominant over the owner. A curious situation may develop. Some owners are unaware of their dogs' perception of their relative status in the household. These are the owners who get a shock when, seemingly out of the blue, the dog reacts aggressively. From the dog's point of view, a well-established subordinate has suddenly behaved quite inappropriately. The subordinate may, for instance, have tried to turn him off a chair or told him to stop barking. The dog's aggression in these circumstances is a reminder to the owner to behave properly. Some owners feel, if their dogs turn on them in this way, that the dogs have stopped loving them and have 'turned against' them. While this is a natural reaction, it is not entirely fair. The dog is behaving more like a Victorian father, who loves his family but must be stern with them if they question his position.

It is only some dogs who are preoccupied by dominance in this way. Dominance is more likely to be shown by male dogs and it is also more likely in breeds of dog in which some aggression is desirable, such as guard dogs. These dogs obviously have to be handled in a special way, if they are not to make life in the household impossible (see Chapter 9). For many owners, part of the pleasure of owning a dog lies in giving him what he asks for. The needs of other human family members may seem so complicated and hard to satisfy that it is pleasant to be asked by a dog member for what one can give. A teenager may want an expensive leather jacket or may ask to go to a dubious, unsupervised party. A husband or wife may be sulky or irritable, and refuse to say what the matter is. A dog, on the other hand, tends to want nothing more complicated than for a ball to be thrown. Or when he wants affection, he asks for it openly. Fortunately, most owners can gratify their dogs' demands without misgiving. It is only the few who have dominant dogs who must be careful. The subject of how to treat dominance aggression is dealt with more fully in Chapter 9.

Territory

Wolves have two kinds of territory. In their search for prey, they may move around over a large area, perhaps twenty miles from end to end. The boundary of this territory is marked by urine and faeces, the faeces being deposited on prominent places, like boulders and tussocks of grass. When two packs share the boundary of a territory, intense marking activity goes on. It is constantly patrolled, being marked and re-marked by either side. Within a territory, there is sometimes a smaller home area which is more fiercely defended. Such an area is necessary when there are cubs living in a den with their mother and too small to move around. The defence of territory is the particular responsibility of more dominant wolves. They will do most of the marking at boundaries and will lead the attack on intruders into the home area.

For a dog, the equivalent of this home area is usually the house and garden he lives in. The equivalent of the wider territory is the parks and streets where he is habitually exercised. Some dogs are more territorial than others. Most take a great interest in who visits the house, but some will watch passers-by out of the window and bark furiously at any who show the slightest sign of pausing by the garden gate. This behavioural trait can be a valuable one, a great reassurance for those living alone. But it can get out of hand.

The Webster family had a Dobermann who attacked any stranger who crossed the threshold. If they tried to restrain him, he might turn and snap at them. The only person who could control him was Mr Webster. If a man called to read the gas meter, for example, when Mr Webster was not at home, they had to shout at him through the letter-box that he would have to come back later. Such fierce defence of territory is often linked with dominance in dogs as well as in wolves. Certainly more dominant dogs are harder to control when they do attack strangers.

Preoccupation with the wider territory of the familiar park is, as with wolves, often manifested by frequent urine marking. Again, this seems to be linked to dominance, so that more dominant dogs insist on stopping to mark every few yards. Dominant bitches may also urinate to mark territory. Owners are sometimes alarmed that this frequency of urination may be a symptom of some infection; if a dog or bitch can contain itself for long periods in the house, the frequency is unlikely to be a manifestation of a physical disorder.

Play

Adults dogs often play with each other. This is not another example of neoteny, because adult wolves do the same. It makes them unusual in the animal kingdom, where normally it is only the young of a species who play. Dog owners normally have no difficulty in knowing when their dogs are playing. They may show the characteristic 'play bow' (Fig. 9) which is an invitation to join in. Or they may do more serious things, such as chasing each other, in a different way, with a certain lightness or springiness in their step. Another characteristic of play is that roles switch frequently: the aggressor becomes the victim, then the aggressor again, all in the space of a few minutes.

Perhaps one reason why adult wolves continue to play is that it can have an underlying serious meaning. For example, a dominance challenge by one wolf towards another may be preceded by some weeks of play-fighting between the two. The lesson for dog owners is that they should not ignore the content of their pets' play. Two dogs from the same household often fight in play and clearly derive enjoyment from this game. In many cases, the aggression never escalates beyond that level. In some

Fig. 9 A 'play bow'.

cases, it momentarily becomes serious from time to time: the owners may hear a growl, a yelp and a scuffle in the next room, but when they go to see what is going on, the matter is settled. More rarely, the play aggression develops into a serious situation where one or both dogs may be physically at risk. Owners should not be so preoccupied by this possibility that they constantly intervene and put a stop to enjoyable games, but they should be aware of it. For similar reasons, it is unwise for an owner himself to play 'dominance' games with a dog: tugs-of-war over toys or wrestling games where the dog stands over the owner are not to be encouraged.

5 • *Fear and Stress*

Dogs are often labelled 'neurotic'. I have heard the term applied to a wide variety of unacceptable behaviour, from biting the postman through raiding the rubbish bin to chasing bicycles. It often seems to be used as part of an irregular verb of the form 'my dog is highly strung, your dog is neurotic, his dog is totally out of control'. In fact the term refers only to some kinds of behaviour and it is important that owners recognize these. The term neurotic is properly applied to any behaviour which is motivated by a high level of anxiety or agitation and in addition is maladaptive or counter-productive. If a student who is worried about his exam the next day drinks half a bottle of gin, he is behaving neurotically. If he spends the evening revising, he is not. In the same way, a dog who becomes so excited when his owner picks up his lead that he runs round in circles squealing, making it difficult to put on his lead, is behaving neurotically. The dog who makes a bee-line for the door and sits there wagging his tail in anticipation is not.

Dogs may express their anxiety or agitation in a number of ways, some more easy to recognize than others.

Phobias

Like human beings, dogs can suffer from phobias. A certain amount of fear is necessary to protect us from danger: it is no bad thing for a dog to have some fear of traffic. On the other hand, if a dog is so afraid that he will not willingly walk on the pavement of a busy street, the fear has become maladaptive.

Owners usually know when their dogs are suffering from fear: they may cower or try to escape. If they cannot escape they may tremble, pant or whine. Like human beings, dogs often like to be close to their nearest and dearest when they are afraid. A dog who is afraid of thunderstorms may follow his owner round the house when one is brewing.

How do dogs, or people for that matter, develop such extreme fears? First of all, there is probably an inborn, hereditary element. All animals tend to show fear of unfamiliar things, for instance. Some dogs will be thrown into a panic when a new piece of domestic equipment comes into the house. Certain fears are also typical of certain breeds, which again points to a genetic factor. Labradors seem to develop a fear of sudden loud noises more frequently than other breeds. A fear of men waving things seems more common in border collies.

But most phobias are acquired during the course of the dog's life. According to learning theory, this happens by means of classical conditioning. If a sudden, nasty or painful thing happens to us, we react physically as well as mentally. Our autonomic nervous system jumps into action: our heart thumps, our stomach churns and so on. According to the theory, these physical sensations become conditioned to anything we perceive at the time of the nasty incident, so that in the future any similar stimuli will evoke these physical sensations: these are what constitute fear. In 1920, an American psychologist called Watson claimed to have demonstrated this process in an eleven-month-old baby, Albert. He put a white rat in front of Albert, but when Albert reached to pick it up, Watson made a sudden, loud noise behind his head. When this had been repeated about five times, the boy began to be afraid of the rat. The fear also generalized to other vaguely similar things, like white rabbits and cotton wool. Other experimenters with similar lack of concern for the feelings of their subjects went on to demonstrate a similar process occurring in animals. For instance, cats were put into experimental cages and given electric shocks. Whenever they were put back into the same cages, they became frightened.

This theory is very close to the common-sense view most of us have of how fear is acquired, so that the results of such experiments often seem obvious. So obvious, in fact, that one is almost prompted to wonder about the motivations of the experimenters. In real life, however, it is often hard to square up the facts with this 'common-sense' theory. In both dogs and man, fears are seldom acquired as the result of a single traumatic experience. The following case was an exception.

Bessie, a bearded collie, was brought to me by Miss Bremner, the daughter of the house, a girl in her late teens. Over the past few months, Bessie had developed a terror of going out for a walk in the streets. When her lead was produced, she cowered away; when it was put on, she strained and pulled to get back in the house. All outings were a tug-of-war. She was perfectly confident when out in the country or in a park: it was the streets which bothered her. To begin with, no one in the family had the least idea of how it had started. Because Bessie was most panic-stricken when taken out by Miss Bremner's brother, family suspicions were aroused that he had perhaps lost his temper with her on some occasion: he strenuously denied this. As often happens, it was not until Bessie had improved and everyone had relaxed somewhat that Miss Bremner remembered the relevant incident. Shortly before the fear had developed, they had taken Bessie to a firework display during the Edinburgh Festival. They had gone to Princes Street, where there were huge crowds. A band played the 1812 Overture, plus cannon, rockets and assorted screeches and bangs. Bessie had been terrified, but at the time none of them had made the connection between that incident and her subsequent fear.

Most phobias, however, do not conform to the common-sense theory. They do not seem to develop as the result of a traumatic incident. Some people, for example, are afraid of flying after some horrendous near-miss in an aeroplane; but most people who grip their seats and look tensely into the middle distance on take-off have never experienced any real danger on an aircraft. How does their fear arise?

According to common-sense theory, if you go back into a situation which frightens you and discover there is nothing to be afraid of, you should lose your fear. But many frightened air-travellers, for example, have a dozen completely safe trips behind them: these safe trips have done nothing but increase their fear. What seems to happen is that the experience of fear itself is so unpleasant (churning stomach, pounding heart, mental images of disaster) that nothing bad need happen in external reality in order to make the situation traumatic: the internal reality is bad enough. This phenomenon could be described as 'being afraid of fear'. People normally use this phrase to encourage timorous others: to make them snap out of it. But of course the process is not based on conscious logic and therefore is not something out of which one can snap.

In the same way, there is no use forcing a phobic dog to face his fear. A dog who is afraid of the vacuum cleaner will not be relieved to discover he does not disappear up the tube if you deliberately hoover close to him: he will be terrified out of his wits. Phobias need special planned treatment, not common sense. This treatment is known as systematic desensitization. It is used successfully to treat phobias in people. It is even more successful with dogs, because their thought processes are less complex.

It consists of teaching an alternative conditioned response to the anxiety-producing stimulus: a response which is incompatible with anxiety. In the case of human patients, this response is usually a state of deep relaxation akin to meditation or hypnosis; they are taught relaxation techniques and practise them regularly until they can achieve this state at will. Dogs cannot be taught relaxation in the same way, but they can usually be induced to relax if they are patted and talked to soothingly. Eating is another response incompatible with anxiety: feeding tit-bits can be used to combat anxiety.

The next stage, in both dogs and humans, is to present the patient in a relaxed state with a version of the anxiety-provoking stimulus which is so mild that no anxiety is aroused at all. A dog who is afraid of vacuum cleaners might be cuddled by his owners in the sitting-room and fed tit-bits while someone else upstairs in the bedroom turns on the hoover for five seconds. When it is clear that the patient can tolerate this mild stimulus, the intensity of the stimulus is increased in small stages. For example the hoover might be turned on for ten seconds, then fifteen seconds; the bedroom door might then be opened so that the sound is louder. To be successful, the treatment must proceed so gradually that no anxiety is provoked. Also, over the period that it is in progress, the patient should not be exposed to a full-blown version of the stimulus: this would reinforce the old connection between panic and the stimulus.

Displacement Activities

Dogs can also express their anxiety and agitation in ways which are harder to recognize. A dog who sexually mounts the legs of visitors is not over-sexed: he is agitated. A dog who chews up the cushions when his owner is out is not being naughty: he is very anxious at being left alone.

When zoologists in the 1940s began systematically to observe animal behaviour, they were puzzled to find that animals in the middle of one instinctive sequence of behaviour might abruptly break off and start on another behaviour pattern which was quite pointless and irrelevant. For example, two sticklebacks fighting at the common boundary of their territories might suddenly start to dig

in the river bottom – a piece of behaviour to do with
nest-building, not fighting. They found that these 'displacement activities', as they called them, were usually
performed when the animal was in a state of conflict, when
it didn't know what to do. The sticklebacks, for example,
were most likely to perform a displacement activity at
the common boundary of their territories because, at that
point, their urges to fight the intruder or give way and
withdraw were most evenly balanced: if a stickleback fights
an invader in the centre of his territory, he is not assailed
by doubts of this kind and displacement activities do not
appear.

In the same way, dogs can use all kinds of activities as
displacement activities at times of tension and frustration,
much as we might bite our nails or pace up and down.
They may chew their paws, chase their tails, dig imaginary
holes in the carpet. Two of the most problematic displacement activities are those already mentioned: sexual mounting and destruction. The arrival of a visitor often arouses
conflicting feelings in a dog. He wants to greet newcomers,
but at the same time he feels they are intruders who need
to be seen off the premises. He may express this conflict
in all kinds of peculiar ways: by greeting the visitors in
a frenzied kind of way, by running round in circles or,
more embarrassingly, by mounting them. The agitation
which prompts a dog to disembowel a sofa or chew the
chair legs when the owner is out arises from the fact that
a dog is a pack animal. Unless he has become accustomed
to it, he feels extremely uneasy when he is separated from
the rest of the pack: chewing and tearing at things are
displacement activities arising from this upset.

> Mrs Templeton was an elderly widow who had got
> Trixy, a little mongrel, from the Dog and Cat home. Trixy
> was good company most of the time, affectionate
> and obedient. Mrs Templeton did not go out much and,
> when she did, she usually took Trixy with her. On
> the occasions when Trixy did not come with her,

for instance to church, Trixy became extremely distressed when she realized she was not to be included in
the outing. She twined around Mrs Templeton's feet,
whining and jumping up. Mrs Templeton could hear
her whining as she went down the path. When she
returned, it was to a scene of devastation. Flower pots
had been knocked off the window-sills, cushions pulled
off the sofa and chewed, newspapers shredded, waste-
paper bins emptied. Mrs Templeton tried to prevent this
by putting every loose object away, out of Trixy's reach,
but Trixy always managed to find something. She had
on occasion resorted to shutting Trixy in the lavatory,
but this made Trixy so frantic she could not bear to
do it except in an emergency.

Dogs can learn over-excitement in the same way as
they learn fear: by classical conditioning. For instance,
many of them quickly learn that the sound of the front
door-bell means visitors. The excitement which visitors
provoke becomes conditioned to the sound of the bell.
The learning may generalize other similar sounds, so the
dog may bark when the telephone rings or at ice-cream
van chimes. These dogs often calm down if the bell is
changed, or disconnected, so that visitors have to knock.
But the respite does not last long, because the excitement
becomes quickly conditioned to the new sound.

Chronic Anxiety

So far, isolated episodes of anxiety or agitation in dogs
who are calm most of the time have been discussed. But
there are some dogs who do not just suffer from isolated
symptoms; for them, anxiety seems a way of life. They
may not, for example, suffer from a single phobia only
but are afraid of all kinds of things.

Barney was a black collie–Labrador cross of unremark-
able appearance. His owner, Miss Buchanan, had got
him when he was six months old: there was some
suspicion that his original owners had maltreated him.

Ever since she had known him, Barney had suffered
from a mass of fears. If any sudden noise happened in
the house, for example if Miss Buchanan dropped something, Barney would run away and hide. Noises outside
the house, for example people shouting in the street,
had a similar effect. Persuading him to leave the house
was a major undertaking. This was highly inconvenient, as Miss Buchanan lived in a flat with no garden:
the only alternative was putting out paper for him
to use. He also suffered from more transient phobias of
certain objects in the house, such as a newspaper,
or the table. When he was in the grip of one of these
fears, he would make elaborate detours to avoid the
object in question. Miss Buchanan was very patient with
Barney and took a great deal of trouble with him.
She had managed to cure him of most of the object phobias as they arose, but she had made no impact on
the noise phobia. When I saw her she was beginning to
lose confidence. She felt understandably that the dog
was crazy and she was beginning to wonder whether
she had something to do with that.

Similarly, some dogs seem to spend their waking hours
moving from one displacement activity to another. They
can become like over-sensitive burglar alarms, rushing
about and barking when the front door-bell rings, when
the telephone rings, when the washing machine goes
into fast spin. They may be constantly on the go, under
people's feet, whining and pawing at their owners for
attention. Such anxious dogs can be extremely annoying
to live with, but expressing annoyance with them by
shouting at them will only make matters worse.

Major was an Alsatian belonging to the Murray family.
For Major, the day began at around 5 am, when he
would run up and down the kitchen, whining and
scraping at the doors. If someone did not get up to let
him out, he would mess the kitchen. When the door
was opened he would shoot out of it, but instead of
immediately urinating, he would dash round and round
the garden, pausing only to dig up the flower-beds. This
pointless activity went on for most of the day. When

he was particularly worked up, he chewed his tail,
which was permanently ragged and scarred.

When a human being develops a neurotic illness, it
is usually as a result of an interaction between the
circumstances in which he finds himself and his own
personality. Some people can cope with life stresses
which would overwhelm others with anxiety. The same
is true of dogs: the external environment and the dog's
own personality both contribute to the development of a
neurosis.

Causes of Neurosis

Single phobias or over-excitement triggered by a specific
situation are very common. In the survey I conducted, I
found that two out of three dogs had an irrational fear of
something. Dogs who have these isolated symptoms are
often perfectly normal the rest of the time.

Dogs such as Barney or Major who have pervasive
neurotic problems are much rarer. The cause of a single
neurotic symptom is often fairly straightforward; the dog
is upset by some unpleasant experience or he is upset
by some neutral event which has become associated by
learning with an unpleasant experience. The causes of
neurotic personality problems are often more complex.

Physical suffering
There is no doubt that cruelty and ill-treatment can damage
dogs psychologically. Owners of problem dogs are often
relieved if they can find some evidence of ill-treatment in
their previous history, because they feel this both explains
the problem and exonerates them. Often, however, in
cases I see, the evidence for cruelty by a previous owner
is scanty. The present owner may infer it from the fact
that the dog draws back when someone raises his voice
to him; this is to argue backwards.

Some physical ill-treatment is probably more shocking

to us than it is to dogs, who cannot appreciate the degree of the owner's responsibility. They can probably survive starvation or a dirty, flea-ridden coat without undue psychological trauma. Paradoxically, inconsistent ill-treatment is probably more harmful than consistent cruelty (see the section on conflict below), which is why dogs who have been rescued by the RSPCA may go on to make acceptable pets.

On the other hand, some medical conditions can produce more prolonged and continuous suffering than most cruel owners can be bothered to inflict. This can certainly cause neurosis, especially if it occurs early in life.

> Prince was an eighteen-month-old Alsatian owned by a young couple, Mr and Mrs Paterson. When he was a puppy, he had developed panosteitis, a rare condition causing bone inflammation. This lasted about a year, until it resolved spontaneously, but during that time, most movements caused Prince great pain. Mr and Mrs Paterson nursed him lovingly and conscientiously, travelling regularly to the Glasgow Veterinary School for expert advice. When he had made a full physical recovery, however, it became obvious that psychologically Prince was far from well. He seemed afraid of his owners, preferring to spend his time crouched in a far corner of the room behind a sofa. If he was allowed to, he spent most of his time in the garden, keeping his distance from the back door. To an observer who did not know his history, it would have looked as if his owners monstrously ill-treated him.

Loss

This is another kind of event which owners usually recognize as being potentially traumatic. When people suffer a serious loss, such as the death of a close relative, a period of numbness is usually followed by a period of intense anguish and anxiety. During this time, the bereaved person may feel as if they are searching, actually or metaphorically, for the lost relative. This state eventually gives way to hopelessness and depression. If all goes well, the bereaved person gradually emerges from this state to resume a normal life; but if there are other complicating factors it can happen that this normal mourning process becomes stuck and the bereaved person does not return to proper functioning.

The same thing can happen with dogs. As already mentioned, temporary separation from the owner can evoke intense short-term anxiety. If they lose their owners permanently, most dogs eventually adjust and settle down in new surroundings, but for some the experience has a more lasting effect. The psychoanalyst Bowlby showed that human children under the age of five are particularly vulnerable to separation from those they rely on. In the 1940s he observed children admitted to hospital for minor operations such as tonsillectomy. In those days, parents were not normally admitted with their children, nor were they allowed unrestricted visiting. In such circumstances children showed all the signs of a bereavement reaction: protest, followed by despair. He also found that even a week's separation under such circumstances had a long-term effect on these children.

In the same way, young dogs seem especially vulnerable to separation. It makes them more anxious and clinging in later life. Research has shown that dogs acquired from animal shelters are more likely to show destructive behaviour in the owners' absence, for which the most probable explanation is that the changes of ownership induce in some dogs a profound sense of insecurity, so that they cannot cope with even temporary absences of someone they have become attached to. Dogs can also be affected by the loss of other dogs.

Archie was a young Labrador owned by Mrs Anderson. At the time she first got him, at eight weeks old, she had another Labrador called Hamish. Archie was extremely attached to Hamish: he was his 'sun, moon and stars' according to Miss Anderson. When Archie was six months old, Hamish died. The effect on Archie was profound. He was miserable, withdrawn and would not eat. During this time, Miss Anderson happened to take him on a long car journey. He slept, until a heavy shower came on, when he was woken by the sound of the rain drumming on the car roof. Miss Anderson described how he seemed for a moment bewildered and then was seized with terror. He leapt on Miss Anderson's lap, then tried to twine round her legs, nearly causing an accident. Shortly after this, Miss Anderson bought another dog and Archie's depression was cured. However, he was left with a lasting phobia: every time it rained on a car journey, the original scene of terror would be re-enacted. It was for this that Miss Anderson was seeking treatment.

Conflict

Conflict – the experience of being pulled two ways in a situation, of feeling one should do something but not knowing what to do – is a powerful generator of anxiety. We have already seen how blowing air in a cat's face can make it neurotic and how similar circumstances can produce fits in rats. An associate of Pavlov, Shengar-Krestovnikova, showed that conflict without any punishment can also produce a breakdown. In her experiment, a dog was conditioned to salivate when he was shown a circular shape by repeatedly giving him food straight afterwards. On other occasions, he was shown an oval shape, but food never accompanied the oval and he learned not to salivate on those trials. The next step was to make the oval more and more similar to the circle, so that eventually the dog was faced with a shape which he could not categorize as an oval or a circle. At that point he broke down, yelping, trembling and trying to escape. What is more, this agitated state lasted long after the experiment had ended.

In a pet dog's life, the most important potential source of conflict is his owner, who often does not realize what a profound effect he is having on the dog. This is partly why punishment is such a risky business; it can give rise to a conflict between fear of, and attachment to, the owner. But, as we have seen, punishment does not need to be involved in order for a conflict to produce powerful anxiety. Mere inconsistency can be stressful for a susceptible dog. For example, when the owner is in a relaxed frame of mind, he may enjoy his dog jumping up on him in welcome; when he is preoccupied, he may find the same behaviour very annoying. Most dogs can read their owner's body-language well enough to be able to predict what kind of response is likely, but if an owner is unpredictable or if his moods change without warning, this can be stressful for the dog. The dog may also be in conflict if there is disagreement among family members about what he should and should not be allowed to do: for example, some of the family may cuddle him when he jumps up beside them on the sofa, whereas others may shout at him if they find him on the furniture. This is why extremely agitated dogs are often found in families where there is stress and upheaval.

> Mrs Campbell telephoned me about Cindy, a whippet cross. She had taken Cindy to the vet for euthanasia but he had refused to destroy a healthy animal, insisting that she consult me first. When Mrs Campbell came to see me the first time, she brought her six-year-old daughter. Both she and her daughter looked pale and tense, with dirty, straggly hair. The child whined and clamoured for her mother's attention to such an extent that she was not able to give me a coherent story. I tried giving the girl a pencil and paper (a veterinary consulting room has limited resources for entertaining children) but that did not hold her attention for long. Finally it became too much for Mrs Campbell and she suggested we postpone the interview. The dog lay peacefully on the floor throughout.
> When she came to see me again, she had only the dog and this time she was able to tell me about the problem. Cindy chewed up things in the house: books, toys, the carpet, the table legs, anything she could

find. What was very unusual was that she did this not
when Mrs Campbell was out but when the family was at
home. She was apt to sneak away into another room,
often into the children's bedroom, to find something
to chew. It eventually emerged that she was particularly
liable to do this when there was some kind of row
or disturbance going on between the human members of
the family. It seemed that these disturbances happened
fairly frequently: Mrs Campbell admitted she was at
her wits' end with the children. She had three girls and
all were showing behavioural disturbance of some kind,
bed-wetting, hyperactivity and so on. The marriage was
also clearly in great difficulties, with her husband saying
he could not stand it much longer. It seemed clear
that Cindy's unusual behaviour was a direct result of all
this family upheaval.

Personality

There is no doubt that some dogs are more susceptible to
developing neurosis than others. As has been pointed out,
early loss or separation can make a dog more vulnerable.
Other disturbances in early life can also predispose a dog to
anxiety. For example, experimenters have reared puppies
in isolation from the world, in bare boxes, without any
contact with other dogs or with human beings. When these
dogs emerge from their isolation, they may show all kinds
of disturbed behaviour. They may be terrified of everyday
objects. They may dash to and fro in a frantic way.

In real life, not many puppies are reared in such conditions of extreme sensory deprivation. Some, however,
are reared in situations bad enough to affect them permanently.

Heather was a bearded collie owned by Mr and Mrs
Hall, a middle-aged couple. (It is no coincidence that
two of the neurotic dogs in these case histories were
bearded collies: they have a particularly bad track record
in this regard.) Mr and Mrs Hall were both psychiatric nurses. They realized that Heather was rather like
some of their human patients and treated her with

great tolerance. She was lucky: many owners would
have lost patience with her. They had got her when she
was twelve weeks old from a farmer. She and the
other puppies had been reared in a barn, visited only by
the farmer's daughter who brought them their food.
When Heather first arrived, she was terrified of Mr Hall.
She cowered away and would not go near him. She was
also very nervous and fearful in the house. Any sudden
noise, like the curtains being drawn, would send her
rushing to another room. To cap it all, she was nervous
of going out as well. By the time I saw them, Mr
Hall had managed to gain her confidence and they had
managed to coax her out to the back garden to relieve
herself. Any sudden noise, however, sent her rushing back into the house. They could sometimes persuade
her to go for a walk when the streets were deserted,
but the sight of a stranger, even at the other end of
the street, made her turn and run for home in a panic.

There are also inherited personality factors in neurosis.
In the 1960s, an experimenter called Oddist Murphree
developed, by selective breeding, two strains of pointer:
one normal and the other nervous and fearful. The puppies
from the neurotic strain behaved differently from the
normal puppies on experimental tests such as reaction
to loud noise. These differences showed clearly as early
as two months after birth and started to appear after only
one generation of selective breeding: in other words, the
mating of two neurotic pointers produced noticeably more
neurotic offspring.

Owners often attribute neurosis to inbreeding; the
experiment does not support this notion. In Murphree's
study, his normal strain of pointers were as inbred as his
neurotic ones. It was the personality characteristics of the
pairs selected for mating rather than the closeness of their
kinship which was important. That inbreeding itself does
not cause neurosis is demonstrated by the fact that guide
dogs are often very inbred, but in guide dog breeding
programmes only the most stable, reliable dogs are used.

When a predisposition to neurosis is inherited, what is

passed from one generation to the next? At the moment we cannot be certain, but, if we extrapolate from human findings, it seems likely to be a characteristic of the brain and the autonomic nervous system: a tendency to react more emotionally to outside stimuli and to become accustomed to those stimuli more slowly. Experiments with human subjects have shown that if patients suffering from anxiety neurosis are played loud startling sounds over headphones they show exaggerated responses in terms of heart rate, sweating and so on. These responses also tend to occur again and again if the sounds are repeated. The response of normal subjects is less violent in the first place; it also tends to diminish rapidly with repetitions of the sound.

The other interesting question is 'What makes some neurotic dogs behave in a fearful and withdrawn way and others behave in an excitable way?' Again, we can borrow some useful ideas from human psychology. In the 1940s and 1950s, Hans Eysenck, a psychologist working at the Maudsley Hospital in London, developed a scheme for classifying human neurosis. He suggested that people can be divided into two kinds of personalities, introverts and extroverts. Introverts tend to be thoughtful people who plan ahead and have a few close friends. Extroverts are more sociable and impulsive. If people of these two personality types are neurotic, it tends to show itself in different ways. Neurotic introverts develop phobias, hypochondriasis and obsessional symptoms. Neurotic extroverts do not keep their worries to themselves, but act in hysterical and emotionally impulsive ways.

This difference between introversion and extroversion is caused by another underlying difference in the nervous system of the two groups, a difference in learning ability. Introverts acquire classically conditioned responses more quickly, so that introverted neurotics readily acquire fears and phobias. Extroverts acquire these responses more slowly: neurotic extroverts act out their emotions because they have not been conditioned to inhibit them.

Whether this is a useful theory as far as human neurosis is concerned is open to question. Doubt has been thrown on the experimental findings which are supposed to link the extroversion/introversion classification system with underlying physical characteristics. It is also certainly an over-simplification of human personality. It does not begin to do justice to the complexity of the phenomena. Canine neurosis is almost certainly more complex too, but this theory does provide a possible classification framework. There is some evidence from experiments with dogs to suggest that they too can be divided into introverts or extroverts. Extrovert dogs act impulsively: they react positively, whether with friendliness or aggression, towards strangers and strange things. Introverted dogs are more cautious: they take their time to size up a situation. Introverted neurotic dogs are the ones who develop phobias, whereas extroverted neurotic dogs are the ones who get agitated and engage in displacement activities.

If you have a neurotic dog, you are lucky if someone has not suggested to you that it is your fault, and you must be very self-confident if you have not wondered this yourself. Certainly, as we have seen in this chapter, it is possible for an owner to make a neurotic dog worse, for example by exposing him to stress or conflict. But most of the causes of neurosis are beyond an owner's control: you need not blame yourself. On the other hand, there are steps you can take to make life more tolerable for both of you. These are discussed in Chapter 10.

6 • *Psychology of Puppies*

More is known about the psychological development of puppies than about most other animals. This is because dogs are such obliging experimental animals; it is also because of the need to rear reliable guide dogs. It is a pity that these findings are not more widely known and applied by people who breed dogs: it is one of the aims of this chapter to set out the implications of these findings in such a way that they can be applied practically. The chapter does not deal with the physical aspects of breeding and puppy rearing, only the psychological aspects.

It is a commonly held view among breeders and vets that ordinary owners should not dabble in breeding: that allowing your pet bitch to have one litter is an ill-conceived venture. Obviously there are points in favour of leaving it to the more experienced. With bitches and owners who have had more than one litter, things tend to go more smoothly. On the other hand, amateur owners who are prepared to take trouble can rear lovely puppies. It should be said in favour of the dabbling owner that he is less likely to rear the puppies in a shed at the end of the garden; the event is special for the whole household and the puppies are more likely to spend their early weeks in the bosom of the family, receiving individual attention. As will be seen later in the chapter, this is extremely important.

Amateurs, therefore, should not be deterred from breeding, provided they are prepared to spend time and take trouble. It is a shock to many people to discover that puppies can be as time-consuming as babies; more of a tie, even, because they cannot be taken around in carry-cots. Fortunately, they do not take so long to grow up.

Nor should prospective owners be deterred from buying amateur puppies. The main risks of inexperience are physical. First-time breeders probably lose more puppies at birth and in the early weeks. The puppies who have survived to eight weeks are probably a better bet than the mass-produced variety.

Mating

When arranging for puppies to be brought into the world, it should always be borne in mind that there is already a surplus. Pure-bred puppies have the best chance of homes; in any case, prospective breeders should always research their market first; preferably they should have buyers lined up. It is usually recommended that the owner of the bitch should go to a professional stud: the practice of allowing her to get together with a friend's nice dog is generally frowned upon. Certainly there are advantages to a professional stud. He probably knows what he is doing and it is much more likely that a successful mating will take place. On the other hand, the bitch's owner is in a better position to assess the temperament of a friend's dog; it is difficult to find out much about the temperament of a professional stud. The fact that he has done well in the show ring only demonstrates that he has not got a phobia of crowds and does not bite judges regularly.

Pregnancy and Delivery

If behavioural changes occur during pregnancy, they are likely to be positive: the bitch may be more affectionate, for example. As the delivery day approaches, she is likely to wander around, worrying about where she is going to have the puppies. The owner will already have worried about the same thing. The ideal location is a place where the bitch can have space and privacy, but which is also handy for the owner to visit. But when the owner has decided on the preferred spot, he must be prepared to be flexible. The bitch may well have her own ideas and a head-on confrontation is likely to be counter-productive. Some bitches who are used to sleeping on the owner's bed are quite happy to move into the box-room when the puppies arrive. Others are not. Obviously the bitch cannot be allowed to wander at will outside, and have her puppies under the toolshed, but it is often a workable policy to allow her (within reason) to have her first puppy where she feels most comfortable, then move that puppy to the chosen location. The bitch will usually follow.

It used to be recommended that whelping boxes be of a clinical design – shallow open trays – so that the owner could see what was going on. These were lined with disposable paper and heated from above by an infra-red lamp. At about the same time that human mothers were arguing that hospitals are, psychologically speaking, not the best place to have babies, breeders started to realize that bitches tended to be less anxious if they were provided with something more similar to the den or hole in the ground which they would use in the wild state. Bitches often feel more secure in a box with sides, a top and a small entrance hole: the top and sides should be removable so that the owner can see what is going on when he needs to: during whelping, for example (Fig. 10). Heating is best provided by insulation round the box and a heating pad under part of the floor of the box. The bitch can then lie on a cooler part, but the puppies can crawl on to the heated part if they want to.

Bitches have an inherited set of instinctive behaviour patterns to take them through the delivery and rearing of their puppies. It may not be a complete or perfect set, however, especially in domestic bitches. If the owner is concerned about the survival of the puppies and, indeed, about the safety of the bitch, he must be ready to intervene

Fig. 10
An enclosed box for a bitch with puppies.

tactfully should the need arise. For example, just after delivery, the bitch ought to be able to remove the foetal membrane, bite through the puppy's umbilical cord and lick him clean and dry. But some bitches look confused and do nothing, especially if it is the first puppy of a first litter: the owner must be on hand with a pair of scissors and a towel to do it if necessary.

The new-born puppy has a limited repertoire of simple behaviour patterns which, when things go well, fit in with those of the bitch. When he is cold or hungry, he can yelp. He can also crawl forward until he encounters a nipple-like object: this elicits sucking and kneading the breast with the forepaws. For her part, the bitch reacts with concern if she hears her puppies yelping. She also instinctively lies down with her legs stretched out, forming a kind of funnel to guide the puppies to feed (Fig. 11).

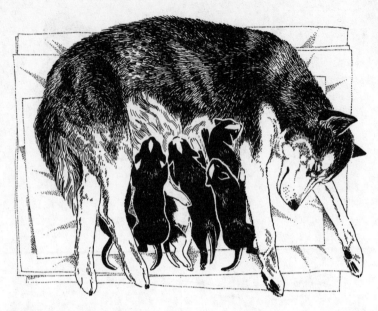

Fig. 11
Instinctive behaviour:
a bitch nursing puppies.

She licks the puppies continually, waking them to feed and stimulating reflex urination and defecation.

This system works pretty well, for most puppies, but it is a mindless system on both sides. Puppies can get lost or squashed and there is no mechanism for ensuring that smaller, weaker puppies get special attention. In fact, the bigger puppies tend to push them away from the best teats and a downward spiral may set in. The situation should therefore be constantly monitored, especially as there is evidence that, in pigs, protein deficiency just after birth can produce hyper-active, anxious adults. Even if the runt of the litter survives physically, there may be a higher chance of his being neurotic in personality. Owners should therefore be ready to step in and give supplementary feeding to a puppy who is not gaining weight at the same rate as the others.

Puppies have the best chance of thriving if their mother

spends as much time with them as possible. The bitch should instinctively do this, but her instincts may need to be fostered. She should not be encouraged to spend time away from her puppies, going for walks or looking for company elsewhere. Some bitches get lonely and desert their puppies to be with the owner. To shut her in with them can make her more upset. The solution may be for the owner to spend more time in the puppy room or to move the puppies into a less isolated room.

Many bitches are defensive of their litters, growling when people, especially strangers, come near. This is normal and should not be discouraged. Even bitches who do not show this protective aggression should not be exposed to casual visitors.

Psychological Needs

Until they are two to three weeks old, puppies are comparatively isolated from the outside world. They can neither hear nor see. Although they can feel cold and hunger and tactile sensations, their nervous systems are not properly developed. EEG recordings of electrical activity in the brain show a pattern characteristic of sleep all the time, even when they are moving and feeding. Their needs are correspondingly basic and primitive, food and warmth being the main ones. The owner's role during this time is therefore to see that these needs are met, preferably by the bitch.

Between two and three weeks of age, the puppy changes dramatically. From being at the behavioural level of, say, slugs, in a matter of days the puppies start to show all the behavioural complexities of one of the higher mammals. As soon as they are able to see, hear and walk, they begin to respond to each other, the mother and the owner as fellow-creatures. They begin to play with each other and to be lonely when they have no company. Psychologically, the next ten weeks are critical in the puppies' lives. Their experience during this time will fundamentally affect their personalities.

To start with, during this time they learn whom to regard as a member of the same species. Plenty of contact with human beings during this time ensures that they are regarded as honorary dogs, so that the puppy will form proper social relationships with them.

If a puppy has no contact with people at all before he is three months old, he will behave like a wild animal. He will be afraid of human contact and certainly will not be prepared to accept a human being as a pack leader. Limited contact with people before that time improves matters a bit, but it has been shown that guide dogs reared in kennels until they are fourteen weeks old do less well than those who go to live in a household at an earlier age. In the same way, if a puppy meets cats at this age, he will be more inclined to live amicably with them later on.

Puppies also learn from their litter-mates during this period. They spend a great deal of time playing together, which seems to enable them to develop and refine instinctive patterns of behaviour. A puppy who has gone to his new home too early, before the age of six weeks, say, may have difficulties in his interactions with other dogs in later life. It is as if his body-language is not subtle enough to cope with certain situations. A common problem is that these dogs get into fights with other dogs, not because they are abnormally aggressive, but because they do not seem to know how or when to behave submissively. They may also have sexual difficulties. These dogs may not seem to know which end of a bitch is which, or they may attempt to mount from the side.

It is probable that interation with their mother is important too. Experiments with mammals such as monkeys and rats have shown that if young animals are isolated from their mother, they show deficiencies in caring for their own young.

Puppies also learn a great deal about their physical surroundings. As was seen in Chapter 5, rearing dogs in simple, boring environments can produce a neurosis in which the dog is afraid of anything he has not encountered in these early weeks; Heather, the bearded collie, who spent the first twelve weeks of her life in a barn, was afraid not only of strange people, but of ordinary household noises and of the world out of doors. Furthermore, experiments have shown that these deprived dogs are not only emotionally unstable, they also show deficiencies in the ability to learn. It seems that the modern recommendations to improve your baby's IQ by hanging mobiles round the cot also apply to puppies.

This phenomenon – the limited time in a puppy's life during which psychological experience is crucial – is not confined to dogs. It is a common feature of the development of most young animals and is known as 'the sensitive period'. What brings it to an end is the emotion of fear. This develops gradually from five weeks to twelve weeks. At five weeks, a puppy will approach most new things and people with confidence, eager to investigate. As the weeks go by, this approach tendency tends to be tempered more and more by caution. A puppy who met a cat for the first time at five weeks old would probably go up to it to get better acquainted. If this first meeting took place when he was twelve weeks old, he might well run away.

Recommendations for Breeders and Owners

These findings have implications for the way puppies are brought up, both before and after they go to their new homes. From the age of three weeks, they should not be kept in seclusion. They should be somewhere where they can see and hear normal domestic life. They should also be introduced to a wide range of people, including men and children.

Keeping puppies in an outhouse may be more convenient, but it simply will not do. It may not be practicable to
have seven Afghan puppies in the kitchen all the time,
but conscientious breeders will operate a rota. They will
also give 'puppy parties', with as heterogeneous a human
guest list as possible.

Puppies should be introduced to life outside the house
as well. It is unfortunate that most immunization programmes at the moment require that they should be isolated from possible infection during the whole of the
socialization period. However, they can still be taken for
car rides and carried in the owner's arms when she goes to
post a letter. One friend of mine introduced her puppy to
the High Street by taking him for walks in the pram along
with the baby. This arrangement might not suit everyone,
but it certainly is worth taking some precautions of this
kind: it is a kind of psychological immunization. Many
dogs I see who have problems in the car, for example
trembling or car sickness, have been introduced to the
car relatively late in life. Likewise, many dogs who are
terrified of traffic have been brought up in the country.

The age at which a puppy should go to his new home is
a controversial point. Certainly he should not go before the
age of eight weeks, in order to give him enough time with
his mother and litter-mates. Some animal behaviourists
who have made a study of dog development argue that
twelve weeks is the natural time for a puppy to make the
transition. At that age, in natural conditions, he suddenly
becomes much more independent of his mother: he does
not follow her around but starts to explore and hunt on his
own. Also, his sleep pattern changes so that he does not
have a regular wakeful period during the night. Twelve
weeks would not be a popular age of departure for most
breeders, however: they usually like to be rid of their
puppies by eight weeks. Keeping six Labrador puppies
for an extra month is not something to be undertaken
lightly from the point of view of expense, if nothing else.

Moreover, it may be an advantage for puppies to become attached to the family they are to live with before the socialization period is over. Added to which, it is easier for the owner of one puppy to innoculate it 'behaviourally'. An outing with a litter of puppies in a car (or in a pram) would be quite an undertaking. There is therefore no single ideal age for puppies to leave home. The best time varies for each individual, depending on the circumstances of his breeder and prospective owner.

7 • *Owner Attitudes*

Do you share your bed with a dog? I bet your reaction to that question was not a neutral one. If you *are* in the habit of letting a dog into bed with you, you probably feel a bit embarrassed about it, maybe even guilty; in any case it is not something you would admit to anyone. On the other hand, if you do not have a dog or if you do not allow him in the bedroom, you may well feel disgust at the very idea.

The reason for introducing this intimate topic here is to show how dogs can stir up strong feelings in people. On the face of it, having a dog in bed with you would seem to be a matter of straightforward personal preference. There are reasons for welcoming a dog into one's bed: warmth, companionship, protection or the dog's own preference. There are also reasons why one might not want him there: he might be smelly, dirty, restless and take up too much room. But the whole question stirs up resonances which go beyond a mere weighing up of pros and cons.

All through the ages, dogs have acted as magnets for powerful emotions. On the one hand, they may be symbols of love and trust. According to Virgil, Aeneas's dog, Argus, waited twenty years for him to return from Troy. He was the only creature to recognize Aeneas when he came home in disguise: the joy was too much for the dog and he died. Twenty-five centuries later, the Skye terrier, Bobby, passed into legend when he stayed by his master's grave in Edinburgh's Greyfriars Kirkyard for fourteen years. When I was a schoolgirl, the fictional rough collie, Lassie, had rows of us sitting in the cinema sobbing pleasurably as we watched her travelling hundreds of miles and overcoming extraordinary difficulties to be reunited with her young owner, Johnnie. All these dogs are symbols of fidelity. One of the most worrying questions in human existence is whether those we love will continue to love us when we are separated from them by time, by distance or by death. All these dog legends give a reassuring answer.

Dogs who embody positive emotions tend to be small or long-haired (i.e. cuddly). Frightening ones tend to be larger and belong to one of the guarding or fighting breeds; they may even be wolves, as for example in Little Red Riding Hood. These dogs are aggressive and threatening in a particularly alarming way: they use their mouths and their teeth to attack. The significance of this will be returned to later. Another kind of negative attribute is often embodied by middle-sized, unattractive mongrels. These often have neither name nor owner and appear on the periphery of stories, symbolizing dirt, mess and the breakdown of the social order. For example, a small spaniel takes this role in J. G. Farrell's novel, *The Singapore Grip*: in the confusion which precedes the Japanese invasion of Singapore in 1942, the dog appears and attaches itself to one of the central characters, the Major. It is dirty, repulsive and diseased but it follows him tenaciously.

Because of what dogs mean to people, people are predisposed to think that dogs possess supernatural powers: they are biased towards interpreting a dog's behaviour in this light. For example, dogs feature in ghost stories, either as ghosts in their own right, or with the ability to see ghosts, as in Coleridge's 'Christabel':

> Sir Leoline, the Baron rich
> Hath a toothless mastiff bitch;
> From her kennel beneath the rock,
> She maketh answer to the clock.

Four for the quarters and twelve for the hour;
Ever and aye by shine and shower
Sixteen short howls not over loud;
Some say she sees my lady's shroud.

In order to appreciate some of the psychological functions of real dogs in people's lives, it is useful to look more
closely at the function of these fictional dogs. This appears
most clearly in the more primitive stories: legends and fairy
stories. Fairy stories are especially riveting in childhood,
a time of life when one is learning to make sense of the
world around one and to manage one's own emotions.
They provide a reassuring certainty: a black and white
separation of good and evil. One of the great problems
for young children is dealing with the fact that the people
they love most, their parents, are the same people whom
they hate most: who get angry with them, who deny them
what they want, who are not there when they need them.
One way of coping with these ambivalent feelings is to
split them and feel them about different people: to love
one parent and hate the other, for example. Fairy stories
are full of such splits: good fairies and bad witches, for
instance. The good dogs in legends ancient and modern
have the same property as these good fairies: they are
unreal, possessing only positive attributes. Lassie is only
loved and missed: she does not bite the postman or mess
the carpet.

Dogs are such popular embodiments of feelings of love
and dependency because in reality they are so affectionate
and demonstrative. Also, they express their love physically
and uncritically. A dog does not care if his owner is old or
shabby or smelly. Many adults have not experienced this
unconditional love since they were children. No wonder
a dog can stir deep feelings in them.

But, as has been seen, fictional dogs can also be completely 'bad': vicious and attacking or disgusting and poll-
uting. They are used to represent these qualities because

they sometimes really possess them. Dogs can attack people, they foul footpaths, they carry fleas and worms; they scavenge in rubbish bins and eat rotting carcases. These 'bad' dogs carry such an emotional charge because, like the wish to love and be loved, these 'bad' impulses are also basic human emotions. Although babies experience total bliss (when they are in their mothers' arms after a feed, for example), at other times, they are overwhelmed by feelings of rage and despair: when they are lonely, or hungry and mother does not come.

At this early stage, these emotions are closely bound up with the digestive system. A very hungry baby experiences hunger as gnawing away inside him: when he does feed, he greedily attacks the breast or bottle, sometimes so fiercely that he cannot drink properly. He has no clear sense of the boundary between himself and the world around him: a gnawing hunger pang is not felt as his own sensation but as something alien attacking him.

A small child can easily conceptualize his own anger as a fierce monster, separate from himself. 'Bad' dogs in fairy stories often act as such representations of a child's angry feelings. Little Red Riding Hood is angelically helpful and caring towards her grandmother, trekking through the forest with a basket of food for her. Her resentful feelings are split off and expressed by the wolf, who, so far from feeding Granny, eats her. (But the connection between 'good' Little Red Riding Hood and the 'bad' wolf is indicated by the fact that Little Red Riding Hood is responsible for the wolf's attack on Granny, in that it is she who, in defiance of the instruction not to speak to anyone, tells the wolf where she is going.) This split-off aggression becomes more and more dangerous: it threatens to destroy Little Red Riding Hood herself as she is attacked by the wolf. The story, like other fairy stories, has a reassuring end, as powerful father steps in and gets a grip of matters: he kills the wolf.

Messing and soiling is another kind of aggression important to babies and children. It can be immensely satisfying to be rid of waste products, but, as babies quickly discover, it causes consternation in adults when it happens at the wrong time or in the wrong place. From early on, human beings feel they have this frightening power to spoil things, to create mess and anarchy. 'Dirty' fictional dogs represent this impulse, again split-off: no human being is responsible for them.

The technical name for this psychological process of managing problematic feelings by attributing them to someone else is 'projection'. The use of fictional dogs as objects for projection is obvious. It is often less obvious when real dogs are used in the same way, but it happens, nevertheless. Both collectively in our culture and individually, dogs are often not just medium-sized domesticated carnivores, but lightning conductors for all kinds of feelings.

Dog-lovers are often caricatured and ridiculed – the rich fat lady with her Pekingese on a silken cushion, or the bossy Mrs Antrobus of the Archers, with her Afghans – but let us start with the dog-haters, as they do not have the spotlight on them so often.

There are two kinds of anti-dog people – those who hate dogs and those who fear them. Some of the haters are to be found in pressure groups campaigning for such measures as the exclusion of dogs from parks and beaches. Although some of these demands seem reasonable enough (who enjoys treading in dog faeces?), their literature shows that their dog is a monstrous Little Red Riding Hood wolf, not a real dog. For example, they are preoccupied by the danger of dog bites. These are not pleasant, of course, but the reality is that they are seen less often than human bites in hospital casualty departments. Dog bites are not as dangerous as human bites, either: they tend to make a clean wound, whereas human teeth tend to break off and leave bits behind, causing infection. They are also preoccupied by the risk of disease: toxicara canis is a favourite. Here is the 'dirty' dog fantasy. The fantasy is based on the reality that the condition can indeed be passed on to human beings via the eggs of the roundworm after they have developed in the soil for several months. If the eggs are eaten by children, it is possible for the larvae which grow from them to migrate round the body, more specifically into the eye, sometimes causing visual impairment. However, the reality is also that the condition is very rare. In Scotland, in 1986, three cases were reported. Meningitis was a hundred times more common: 315 cases were reported.

These dog-haters are adopting the same psychological posture as Nazis or National Front supporters. They are holding an easily identifiable and relatively vulnerable section of the population responsible for a great deal of the ills in society. In this connection, it is interesting that the anti-dog pressure groups seem to adopt tactics similar to political groups advocating human persecution. Their public literature is on the whole rational in tone, but they surreptitiously promulgate material which is extreme and emotive: posters with grotesquely drawn dogs defecating or snarling, urging such courses of action as 'Crucify a Dog for Easter'.

Then there are the dog-phobics. These are people who are terrified when a dog comes near them, even if the dog is obviously friendly. They are often aware that this fear is irrational, that the probability of being harmed by a dog is small, but the fear is not based on reason. The following incident features both dog-phobics and dog-haters.

> A reporter, Miss Milne, came to interview me about my views on the right of council house tenants to keep dogs. In an Edinburgh Council estate, there was a rule forbidding dogs. For many years it had not been enforced and a dog population had gradually built up. This estate was beset by social problems: drug abuse, theft, vandalism, etc. Malnourished dogs were to be seen roaming around, fouling the lifts and looking for edible rubbish. The local council, in the face of this appalling situation, had apparently decided to put a

stop to the one thing they had any power to stop:
dog ownership. This was creating a great deal of distress
to conscientious owners, many of whom valued the
protection their dogs afforded against the drug-abusers
and burglars.

The reporter had been fired with indignation when
she heard about the situation and had taken it up
as a personal crusade. While I was talking to her, I
mentioned that I saw human as well as animal patients.
'Oh, do you really?' she said. 'Then perhaps I can
tell you about this dreadful fear I have.' She went
on to tell me how she was terrified of strange dogs
coming up to her, even if they were small and obviously
friendly. She could not convince herself that they would
not suddenly bite her. This complicated her task of
gathering material for her article. When she visited the
housing estate to interview dog-owners, she first had
to brave the neglected strays roaming around the streets
looking vaguely menacing. Even inside a house, there
was the ever-present danger of being introduced to the
occupant's beloved pet. She told me she had not always
been afraid of dogs. About two years before, her boy
friend had left her, refusing to give any explanation. She
had felt very confused and despairing. It was in the
months following his departure, while she was feeling at
her worst, that the fear suddenly developed.

Her case had some similarities with that of Archie, the
dog who developed a fear of rain following the death of
the other dog in the house. It seems as if, in both cases,
the unsettled state of mind caused by loss provided a
fertile ground for a phobia to spring up. In the reporter's
case, it also seems likely that the aggression she saw in the
dogs was really her own anger with her boy friend, which
she experienced as overwhelming and uncontrollable. Her
fear of dogs was a way of coping with her fear of her own
murderous rage with her boy friend. Although it was
inconvenient to have to avoid dogs, it felt less painful
and dangerous than facing how she felt about her boy
friend.

This is the same method as that employed by a baby to

cope with his rage at his absent mother. The local council were also making psychological use of dogs, in the mode of dog-haters. They were escaping their feelings of help-lessness in the face of intractable human social problems by blaming the dogs: you can destroy a dog but you cannot legally execute a drug addict or a burglar.

A phobia of dogs is much more common in children than in adults. It seems to be something which most people grow out of and many former dog-phobics go on to acquire and enjoy their own dogs in later life. Some, like Miss Milne, can appreciate the satisfaction other people derive from dog ownership, even if they themselves do not. Although they suffer more than dog-haters, dog-phobics are in fact less psychologically disturbed. They know that there is something wrong with them; they are in touch with their own feelings to some extent: they experience the fear but not the anger; they are much easier to help, with psychotherapy, for example. Dog-haters, on the other hand, see nothing irrational or abnormal in their feelings: it is extremely difficult to change their views.

Now let us turn to dog-lovers. There are some societies and charities devoted to dog welfare in which the Lassie element is discernible. They tirelessly disseminate infor-mation about dog care, or attempt to re-home unwanted dogs. These are worthy and desirable aims. On the other hand, in their literature there is a flavour of unreality and sentimentality: dogs can do no wrong. For example, they sometimes do not recognize that some dogs, by virtue of their heredity, hormones or early experiences, can never make acceptable pets; that a good home and a loving owner cannot rectify everything. There are other dog welfare and rescue organizations which are more in touch with reality. For example, they assess the temperament of dogs passing through their hands and destroy those who are unmanageably aggressive or destructive.

How about individual dog-owners? Here the stereotypes of fiction do not do justice to the richness and complexity of the meaning of a particular dog to a particular owner. Of course, some owners' dogs do not mean a lot to them. These are often owners who have acquired the dog almost accidentally or on a whim: maybe he was foisted on them by a relative who could not cope with him or a child may have wanted him and has since lost interest. Sometimes he has been bought simply to guard the house. A casual, detached attitude to dogs is not confined to chaotic families living in deprived circumstances. As a child I knew a family whose father was a senior civil servant. They seemed to me normal in every respect, except that, when they went on holiday, they disposed of the dog they had and got a new puppy on their return: it was easier and cheaper than kennelling, I suppose. In a study of fifty dog-owners, I found that owners who were relatively unattached to their dogs tended to have children, whereas those who were extremely attached to them were more likely to live on their own or with just one other person.

Each dog-lover loves his dog in his own particular way, but in this love there is always some element of unreality, of projection. It is this element which makes our own dog seem special: he does not seem like the other dogs you see in the street, he seems almost a person. This form of projection is not the malignant kind practised by dog-haters, the kind which leads to fear or persecution. It is known technically as projective identification: the process whereby one person feels what he imagines another person is feeling. For example, your dog runs expectantly to the door when you get up. You think he wants a walk. You do not particularly want to go for a walk yourself, but in order to please him, you take him out. What is more, so strong is your identification with his feelings, you actually enjoy the outing: you share his pleasure vicariously.

The idea that a satisfactory dog/owner relationship has an element of projective identification is supported by the replies to a questionnaire which I gave to twenty dog-owners. I asked them to rate both themselves and their dogs on a range of adjectives which could apply both to dogs and people, for example 'intelligent', 'nervous' and 'independent'. I found that the people who had problem-free relationships with their dogs tended to see themselves and their dogs as having similar personalities.

This psychological mechanism of projective identification is by and large an extremely helpful one. It enables parents to enjoy feeding and looking after their babies; it enables them to enjoy playing boring, repetitive games with their children. It forms the basis of some of the professional gratification for doctors, nurses and social workers: in caring for others they are vicariously caring for themselves.

But things can go wrong, if the one who is doing the projecting is mistaken about the feelings of the one he is trying to identify with: if he tries to sympathize with the fear of someone who is not feeling afraid, for example. This can happen for two reasons. One is that the object of projection gives signals which mislead the projector. This occurs more easily if the object is a dog than if it is a human being. It was seen in Chapter 4 how an owner can mistake a dog's bid for dominance (for example by placing paws on an owner's knee) for pure friendliness. Misattribution can also occur if the owner's perception is distorted by his own psychological needs and problems. One example of this which I came across involved a dog which did not even exist.

> A woman rang me saying that she had a dog which would not eat. When I asked more about it, she said that the basic problem was that she couldn't see the dog to feed it; it was invisible. It had arrived a couple of days before. She had been sitting on the sofa when she felt it brush against her legs and heard its tail thump against the wall as it wagged it. She described the whole thing so vividly, yet so matter of factly, that I felt the hairs on the back of my neck start to prickle. I wondered if at last I was hearing a real ghost story. But then

she went on to say that she was worried about how to feed this invisible dog. She had become especially worried since the dog had puppies the night before. She had them on the bed and they were only half-invisible (presumably because the father was fully visible): they looked like jelly, you could see through them. This elaboration strained my credulity and I realized that I was dealing with someone who was hallucinating. I asked her if she had had any other strange experiences recently. She said she could see inside the people at her work; she knew which of them were going to die soon, but they were not too pleased when she told them. In fact, she had not been right since her baby had died. He was born with something wrong with him and he had only lived a few days. As she was clearly in need of psychiatric help, I suggested that she tell her own doctor about these odd experiences. She said she would and I hope she did.

Normally it is real dogs who are the recipients of such projections. Most of them are resilient enough to absorb these emotions, but a few are not. Things can then go tragically wrong.

Miss Nesbit, a girl of eighteen, came to see me in despair, two months after the death of her cross-breed, Nobby. She was weepy, she could not eat, she could not sleep, she thought of him constantly. She was contemplating suicide. He had been found abandoned as a four-week-old puppy and she had hand-reared him. She had developed a relationship with him closer than any she had ever known: he instinctively knew what she was feeling. In fact she was in love with him. The trouble was that he was by nature a dominant dog and, at the age of about nine months, he became extremely possessive. The crisis came when she and her best friend Lucy were sitting on her bed gossiping. He suddenly jumped, growling and snarling, at Lucy's face and bit her lip. There was blood everywhere and Lucy had to have stitches. Miss Nesbit felt she had no option but to have Nobby destroyed. She had telephoned the vet immediately: he came and gave Nobby a lethal injection while she held him.

She could hardly bear to talk about the euthanasia, but she thought about it constantly. She also wondered where Nobby was now, how he was feeling and whether, by dying herself, she might be reunited with him. To make matters worse, she felt responsible for his death, because she felt that if she had not been so attached to him, he would not have been so possessive. She could not talk to anyone about her distress: in the circumstances, she could not confide in Lucy. She had tried to explain how she felt to her parents, but they told her not to be silly: they had never liked Nobby in the first place.

If Miss Nesbit had not been infatuated with Nobby she might have been able to control his dominance and possessiveness better, but she had also been very unlucky in Nobby's temperament. This case raises the whole issue of pet bereavement. Miss Nesbit was depressed because of the loss of a loved one: her psychological reaction was similar to those of some people who have lost human relatives. Those who react catastrophically to pet death are often experiencing problems in human relationships: that is why the pet means so much to them. It is a common pattern for a widow to cope 'marvellously' when her husband dies, but to fall apart when her dog dies a year later. The most significant bereavement is the human one, but the grief is not fully experienced until she is alone in the house: the dog's death is the 'last straw'.

What bereaved pet-owners usually need is what most bereaved people need: to talk about their experiences to others who understand. In California, support groups have been set up where mourning dog-owners can do just that. It seems unlikely that this will happen in Britain, at least in the near future. Here such goings-on are generally regarded as embarrassingly excessive.

But to categorize someone as a dog-lover or a dog-hater is often an over-simplification. Some people might be classified as both. The dog press regularly carries stories of people who are prosecuted for neglecting their dogs, but to whom dogs are clearly very important: they may have taken in dozens of strays or be active in the dog-showing world. These are disturbed people who have made dogs the focus of their conflicting emotions.

> One of the most upsetting cases I have seen was a young woman, Mrs Davidson, severely physically handicapped from birth and confined to a wheelchair. She had travelled from Newcastle to see me, expertly mobilizing various agencies in order to make the trip. She whizzed into my consulting room in her electric wheelchair, towing her dog Danger behind her. Danger was a black Labrador-cross with a shifty look: she had got him from the Dog and Cat home about a year before. He made an enormous difference to her life, she said. She had taught him to pick things up for her. I asked her to show me. She dropped a bunch of keys. Danger picked them up and ran into a corner with them. An uneasy silence fell and I asked what the problem was she wanted to consult me about.
> A confused story followed. He had stolen hundreds of pounds worth of meat from the fridge, she said. Her husband was not a dog-lover and was fed up with this. He was even more fed up since Danger had attacked him: Danger had grabbed him by the throat while he was asleep. Also, Danger smelt horrible, she said. But no one else could smell it, not even the vet. Incidentally, the police had been on to her: some silly children were in the habit of trying to pat him and feed him crisps through the bars of her garden fence and one or two of them had had their hands bitten. He wasn't used to children; he sort of lunged at them if he met them in the street.

It was hard to make out the relationship of this account to reality. Some of it seemed downright implausible: it is most unusual for a dog to attack spontaneously a person who is not even moving. There seemed little doubt, however, that this dog was aggressive towards children. Moreover, I doubted the owner had the physical or emotional capacity to understand and carry out a treatment programme, especially as her husband did not seem willing to help.

I said that I did not think there was much I could do for her and that if the dog was really as bad as she was making out, it looked as if he would have to be destroyed. She became very angry at this suggestion, saying that it was against her principles to harm anything, even flies in the kitchen. Danger might be an abandoned stray, but he had a right to live. I suggested that maybe she felt so strongly about this matter because of her own handicaps. She cried and said yes, as a child she had several times overheard people saying it would have been better if she had died at birth. After this she seemed calmer and she left soon afterwards. She telephoned me a week later to thank me and to let me know she had had the dog destroyed. I was not quite sure how I had helped: maybe I had made her feel easier about the euthanasia. In any case, I reflected, I had probably saved a few children's fingers.

A few months later I was at a meeting in Newcastle. Afterwards I chatted to a veterinary nurse who mentioned that she worked in the practice which had referred Mrs Davidson. She also knew Mrs Davidson's next-door neighbour, who had often seen Mr and Mrs Davidson systematically beating the dog. The neighbour had wondered whether to call the RSPCA. The last time I heard of Mrs Davidson was when I read about her in a magazine. She was featured as a brave lady who had triumphed over physical disability and made a career as a dog trainer.

Cruelty towards dogs is also perpetrated by people whose feelings about everyone around them, including dogs, are susceptible to wild fluctuations and are not properly under control. Many mass murderers were sadistic to animals in their childhood. Violence in the family often includes violence towards the animal members of the household. Stuart Hutton, a social worker doing research in this field, has pointed out that this fact can provide a useful early warning system for child abuse. People who are trying to conceal what they have done to a child will often freely admit that they have knocked the dog or cat about: this is more socially acceptable.

Up to this point, the concern has been mainly with the owner's state of mind. But how does this affect the dog? Obviously, if the owner's attitude leads him to ill-treat or neglect the dog, this will do no good to the dog's state of mind or to his behaviour. But the owner's attitude can also affect his dog in much more subtle ways. In each owner's relationship with his dog there is a unique blend of projective identification (feelings which the owner supposes that both he and the dog share, e.g. the need for affection) and projection (feelings which the owner denies in himself but attributes to the dog, e.g. aggression). Many pet dogs are just as much working dogs as are sheep dogs or police dogs: their job is to soak up and remain undisturbed by these projections. If they were not there to fulfil this role, the feelings might be projected on to another member of the household who was less able to cope with them.

Most dogs do this job very well. But sometimes, especially if denied feelings are massively projected on to the dog or if he is neurotic or has a strong urge towards dominance, these feelings are not absorbed: on the contrary, they are reflected back and magnified. Then problems can arise. In the following case, the dog's dominance aggression, combined with the owner's difficulty with her own aggressive feelings, spelt trouble.

> Fanny was a bad-tempered cairn terrier. Her owner, Mrs Finlay, looked nervous and harassed. She seemed nervous of me and over-eager to please: she said 'Yes, yes' to everything I said, almost before I had finished speaking. Mrs Finlay told me that she ran a hotel and the problem was that Fanny was prone to growl and snap when guests patted her. Nobody had been bitten yet, but she dreaded that it would happen. Fanny also had other unpleasant habits. She did not want anyone in the same room while she ate; the kitchen had

to be cleared when she had her meal. Her favourite
resting place was in Mrs Finlay's office, under her
desk. When she was there, Mrs Finlay could not work at
it, because she would try to bite her ankles.

It was clear that Fanny's aggressive behaviour stemmed
from her perception of herself as dominant in the
household. I explained to Mrs Finlay how she should
go about persuading Fanny to adopt a subordinate role
(see Chapter 9). This included preventing those situations
from arising where Fanny was most likely to be aggressive.
It meant giving Fanny her meals off her own territory, in
a strange room. She was to be hand-fed only: Mrs Finlay
was never to put down a bowl of food and leave, but only
to give her food from her own (possibly gloved) hand.
Also she was to block up the opening under her desk,
so that Fanny could not get in there. Mrs Finlay thanked
me profusely for my suggestions but seemed eager to get
away.

When she came again, Mrs Finlay said she was afraid
there had not been much progress. Fanny had been 'very
naughty'. When I questioned her, it turned out that Mrs
Finlay had not really followed the treatment programme.
More particularly, she had not blocked off her desk nor
had she hand-fed Fanny. She said she felt it was not right
to do these things: Fanny was entitled to her privacy.
In order to find a way out of this impasse, I asked her
more about her general situation. It emerged that this
was pretty desperate. Her husband had had a stroke
and needed nursing night and day. She also had the
job of running the hotel now, single-handed. She had
a teenage son, but he never offered to help. She had
asked for her husband to be admitted to hospital, for
rehabilitation or even just to give her a break, but her
GP had dismissed this as unnecessary. Obviously, she
was in a situation in which she was at everyone's beck
and call but felt unable to demand help to which she was
entitled.

One would have thought that, in view of the circumstances, the dog's behaviour would have been the last straw. In a way it was, but at the same time she seemed unwilling to take any definite steps to change it. The clue was in the tolerant way she described Fanny's naughty doings, as if she derived satisfaction from them. In fact, Fanny was doing what Mrs Finlay often wished she herself could do: being cross with people when they approached her, telling them to clear off when she was having her meals or resting. Here the owner's psychological problem made the dog's behaviour worse. Fanny was in reality an aggressive, dominant, dog but Mrs Finlay, for her own reasons, allowed Fanny to get away with it.

Fanny's behaviour eventually improved, but it happened in a roundabout way. I spent a few interviews with Mrs Finlay discussing her general situation. She became more aware that she was feeling hard done by and that this feeling was justified. She became able to ask her son to help out more and I encouraged her to insist on a hospital referral for her husband. As part of this general increase in self-assertion, she was able to be firmer with Fanny. She was able to order her out from under her desk when she wanted to sit there, and she was able to insist on staying in the kitchen during Fanny's meal times, although she still could not go near her. She was less worried about the danger of Fanny biting guests, because she kept Fanny shut in the back premises. She no longer felt that Fanny had a 'right' to wander the hotel at will.

Major, the Alsatian in Chapter 5 whose day was filled with displacement activities like chewing his tail, digging the garden and running round in circles, was a neurotic dog who was vulnerable to his owner's projected conflicts concerning loss and dependency:

> Mrs Murray was a handsome woman in her thirties, well dressed and poised. But, over a few interviews, she told me something of the turmoil which lay below that surface. When Major was a puppy, her husband had

suddenly left her and the children for another woman.
She had felt shattered and for a few weeks had taken to
her bed, unable to face the world. Major had been
a great comfort and a constant companion, cuddling up
with her in bed. Eventually she felt she must pull
herself together and snap out of this. She went to
the other extreme, throwing herself frantically into work
and community activities. She did not like to be at
home for long, because then she began to feel misery
overtaking her. It was at this time that Major's agitated
behaviour began.

It turned out that although Major's behaviour was
seldom normal, he was at his worst when Mrs Murray was
preparing to leave him alone or when he was reunited
with her after a separation. He was at his calmest in
the evenings when she and her children were in the
sitting-room watching television. It also emerged that
Mrs Murray's feelings about Major were intense and
conflicting. At times, she felt very sorry for him. She
read into his disturbed behaviour the same kind of
misery that she had felt when her husband had left.
At these times, she would cuddle him and try to calm
him down. On other occasions, she would be intensely
irritated. He reminded her of difficulties she was trying
to put behind her; he seemed to be trying to keep her at
home and drag her down into her former state of misery.
In these moods, she would shout at him and hit him.

As a puppy, Major had obviously become very dependent on Mrs Murray's company. When suddenly called
upon to adapt to a completely different life-style with
Mrs Murray out of the house a good deal, he could not
cope. Because of her own problems, Mrs Murray could not
deal with Major's disturbance; in fact, she made it worse.

It is sometimes tempting to assume that a dog's problem
must always be due to the owner's psychological difficulties. Novices at dog shows are often advised that their
dogs' fear of the ring or tendency to snap at the judge is due
to 'tension transmitted down the lead'. This explanation

has the advantage that it exonerates the breeder from any responsibility for inherited faults of temperament. Usually, however, the direction of causation is up the lead: a novice dog handler is naturally apprehensive if he knows his dog is liable to do something embarrassing.

Cases like the last two, where the owner's pathology plays such a prominent part, are uncommon, but there are probably many more where the owner's attitude has a more minor role. In a study of fifty dogs and their owners, I asked the owners about their dogs' behaviour and also about their own attitudes towards their dogs; I gave them a questionnaire designed to measure how neurotic the owners were. I found that owners who were extremely attached to their dogs and wanted their dogs to love them and be dependent on them were more likely than average to have problems with dominance aggression. This is presumably because their wish for their dogs' affection prompted them to give the dogs what they asked for, whether it be a pat, food or a game. As was seen in Chapter 4, if a dog is temperamentally inclined to dominance, this kind of behaviour on the part of the owner is likely to encourage him.

I also found that neurotic owners were more likely than average to have dogs who engaged in displacement activities such as sexual mounting of inanimate objects or destructive chewing. As was discussed in Chapter 5, displacement activities are a symptom of stress. Neurotic people tend to subject their dogs to more stress, because they tend to make difficult emotional demands on them; the relationship between Major and Mrs Murray is an extreme example of this.

On the other hand, there was no relationship between a dog's phobias and the owner's anxiety: it seems that fear is not transmitted down a lead. But there was a correlation between an owner's neurosis and the degree to which his dog's phobias were a problem: that is, neurotic owners do not have dogs with more phobias, but they are more upset by the phobias their dogs do have. Presumably neurotic owners identify with the dog's feelings, whereas less neurotic owners are emotionally detached from their dog's behaviour.

What should you do if you suspect that your personality is adversely affecting your dog? It does not make sense to suggest that an owner's personality or even his attitude towards his dog can be changed at will. You cannot feel different or be different to order. But what you can do is become aware of the aspects of your personality and attitude which might affect the dog and try to protect him from them. For example, you cannot alter your preference for a loving, dependent relationship with your dog over a bossy, authoritarian one; nor probably would you want to. But you can, in certain crucial situations, alter your behaviour in order to give your dog the message that you are the dominant person in the household (see Chapter 9). Similarly, neurotic owners cannot choose not to be neurotic and disturbed families cannot resolve their problems just by deciding to do so. But they can become aware of the effect they have on the dog and take steps to protect him from it (see Chapter 10).

> Mrs Ferguson was a small harassed woman in her thirties. She brought her Jack Russell terrier, Flip, to see me because he had developed the habit of running into the sitting-room and chewing the edges of the carpet. But it turned out that this was really a side-show to the main problem in the household, which was the relationship between Mrs Ferguson and her son Billy. Billy was nine and infuriated her by not doing everything he was told. He went out to play before he did his homework and left his room untidy in the mornings. She told me this in tones of deep concern, as if he were shop-lifting or taking drugs. Enormous rows between herself and Billy were routine: she would nag him about his shortcomings until he eventually started shouting at her. It gradually emerged that it was during these rows that Flip would sneak away and start chewing the carpet. (I felt a certain sympathy with this reaction.)

When I pointed this connection out to Mrs Ferguson, she went home and told Billy that he must now certainly do as he was told as his disobedience was driving the dog crazy. When she told me this the next time we met, I explained to her that this was not what I meant: I lowered my sights somewhat. I suggested that she shut Flip away in another room before she tackled Billy or go up and speak to Billy in his room. This she understood and accepted. Also, over the next few interviews, I tried to get her to see that the real problem in the household was not Flip, nor was it Billy: it was the fact that she and Billy were getting on so badly. The solution was not for Billy to capitulate: she and Billy were going to have to get together to work on the problem. She could not accept this at all; she kept reiterating that children must do as they are told. So the problem in the household did not get any better. But the dog's behaviour did improve, because she did get into the habit of protecting him from the rows.

Part II
Problems and How to Treat Them

8 • *Planning Your Treatment*

This and the following three chapters are intended as a DIY guide to treating problem behaviour. This chapter is an overall guide to strategy: how to plan your campaign. Chapters 9, 10 and 11 deal with details of various kinds of problems, details which you should fit into your overall plan.

If some aspect of your dog's behaviour is a problem to you:

DON'T just wait and hope that matters will improve. Certain kinds of problem may improve as the dog matures; for example, puppies who urinate when they get very excited tend to grow out of this habit. But other kinds of problem (e.g. dominance aggression) tend to get worse with age. And, in general, problem behaviour tends to get worse the longer it persists. Even if, having assessed the problem, you decide to leave matters alone for a while, this masterly inactivity will be part of a plan. You will feel better about it than if you just let matters drift.

DO start by making a *diagnosis* and drawing up a *treatment plan*. By making a diagnosis, I mean formulating a theory about why the dog acts as he does. It need not be complicated and it may well turn out to be wrong, but it is like a map made by early explorers. Without it, you will be without direction. Such a theory is what differentiates a scientific from an unscientific way of proceeding. Owners often try to cure a behaviour problem with one remedy after another. Often they have no idea of why the remedy is supposed to work. It may be a herbal remedy which is advertised vaguely as having a beneficial effect on the nerves. Or it may be something like smacking the dog with a rolled-up newspaper, which a neighbour recommends because it cured his dog of the same thing. If these methods fail, owners are no better off than when they started. But if you have a theory which dictates a remedy, even if it fails, you have made some progress, because at least you have disproved your theory.

Suppose, for example, your dog makes a huge puddle in the kitchen every night. You might start with the theory that he does it because he cannot hold on until morning. You therefore take up his water bowl during the evening and walk him last thing at night. If, in the morning, there is still a puddle, but a much smaller one, then a full bladder cannot be the cause. You might then adopt the theory that he does it because he is restless and lonely. So you test that out by allowing him access to somebody's bedroom in the night. The more theories you test, the more you will learn about your dog's behaviour and the nearer you will be to a solution.

While formulating your theory and drawing up your treatment plan, by all means invite the opinions of other people: friends, family, doggy acquaintances. They may have new ideas and fresh light to throw on the matter. Do not be intimidated by other people, however, and do not accept what they say blindly. You may adopt their suggestions as part of your treatment plan, but only if they fit in with your own theory about your dog. Do not be tempted to accept the implication that what worked for Candy the cairn terrier next door will also work for your own Bonzo. Bonzo and Candy may be doing what seems like the same thing, but for quite different reasons.

In canvassing opinions, it is a good idea to *include your veterinary surgeon*. There are a number of reasons why he may be especially useful. For one thing, he may have a particular interest in dog behaviour problems and be able to offer a great deal of help with the diagnosis and treatment plan. He also may be able to prescribe a drug as an aid to treatment, for example to make your dog less anxious or less dominant. In addition, he can check whether there is a physical cause for the problem. It is particularly important to do this if the dog suddenly starts to react irritably when he is handled, as this might indicate that he is in pain; if urination in the house is accompanied by an increase in drinking; if defecating in the house is accompanied by a change in the stools; or if any behaviour problem is accompanied by unsteadiness or loss of consciousness.

Keeping a Diary

Before you decide on diagnosis and treatment, you may find it useful to keep a diary of the problem over a week or two. In it you should record:

1. The time at which the problem behaviour occurs: both the chronological time and the time in relation to the daily routine, e.g. after breakfast. This may help you to pinpoint times at which the behaviour is most likely to occur. You can then concentrate your efforts on those periods of the day.

2. Where the problem behaviour occurs. If you find it happens regularly in the same place, this place may be a triggering stimulus. If aggression always happens in the same place, then consider the possibility that the dog is defending what he sees as his territory.

3. Who else is present. If the dog only engages in the problem behaviour when someone else is present, it is likely that this person is relevant. Maybe the problem behaviour is some expression of the relationship between them (e.g. dominance aggression). Maybe the other person is rewarding it in some way (for example, by paying attention to it).

4. What happens immediately before the behaviour. This might be a triggering stimulus (e.g. someone reaching out to touch the dog might trigger aggression) or it might be a source of stress (e.g., a family row).

5. What happens immediately after the problem behaviour. What the dog does afterwards is not as important as the events which occur around him, including the reactions of other people: they may be rewarding to the dog.

When you are keeping the diary you may well find that there are some questions you cannot answer. For instance, if the problem behaviour occurs when you are out, you may not know exactly when it happens or what immediately precedes or follows it. You should try to fill in these gaps by carrying out experiments. For example, if your dog is destructive when you are out, it is important to know whether he has his chewing binge immediately you leave or after an hour or two. You might check on this by going back to the house ten minutes later or by leaving a tape recorder running.

Diagnosis

In arriving at a diagnosis, you should try to answer the following questions:

1. Has the behaviour an instinctive motivation? For example, is it dominance aggression? Maternal behaviour? Frightened behaviour? A displacement activity? To be able to answer this question you should first of all read the descriptions of various kinds of problem behaviour in Chapters 9, 10 and 11.

2. Is there a learnt component in the behaviour? Is the behaviour sometimes followed by an event which the dog might find rewarding? For example, does it sometimes make you pay attention to him? If so, instrumental learning may be involved. Remember, the reward need not follow the behaviour invariably, or even on most occasions. Intermittent reinforcement can keep behaviour going effectively.

Is the behaviour always triggered by the same kind of stimulus? For example, is barking always triggered by a high-pitched noise or by the car engine starting up? If so, classical conditioning is likely to be involved.

3. Is stress contributing to the problem? This is likely to be so if:

You are regularly hitting the dog or getting cross with him.

You are reacting inconsistently to the dog.

There is some kind of disturbance or upheaval in the household.

Bear in mind that problem behaviour can have more than one cause. For example, it might be an instinctive behaviour pattern which the dog has learnt to perform in a particular situation and stress might also be contributing.

Planning the Treatment

Your theory about the dog's behaviour will determine the form of the treatment. Suggestions about specific treatment methods will be found in Chapters 9, 10 and 11. Here are some general suggestions:

Dominance
Even if your dog is not showing aggression towards anyone, his perception of himself as dominant in the household may be part of the problem. For example, such a dog is often unwilling to do what he is told and therefore harder to control. You should read Chapter 9 and decide whether he shows any of the features of a dominant dog, e.g. an independent life-style. If so, you should increase your dominance over him by the methods described in that chapter. This can do no harm and may well do good.

Punishment

Whatever the problem, if you are punishing the dog or getting cross with him, stop it. It is clearly doing no good, because the problem is still persisting. It may well be making matters worse.

Systematic Desensitization

This is a useful treatment method which can be applied to a range of behaviour problems. First of all, prevent the dog from performing the problem behaviour. If he eats the letters when they come through the door, get the postman to put them in a box outside. If he is liable to chase joggers in the park, do not take him to that park.

Do not worry that this is side-stepping the problem. If response prevention were all that you did, it would be, but as a stage of a treatment programme, it is a positive step. In fact, it is often such an essential step that it is worth going to some trouble to engineer it and putting up with the temporary inconvenience. If the dog goes crazy when the bell rings, it is worth disconnecting the bell. If he is frightened to go outside to relieve himself, provide him with newspaper indoors.

If you think you cannot prevent the problem behaviour because you cannot predict it, try paying close attention to what immediately precedes it. You may well find that you can identify triggering stimuli which you were not aware of before. You may then be able to prevent these stimuli from occurring or take swift avoiding action if they do.

> Mrs Scott had two cocker spaniels, Spot and Smudge, who fought constantly. When she thought about it, she realized that they never fought when she was not in the room; also, if she had just talked to Smudge or patted him, Spot would attack him. Going out for a walk was a risky time; she realized this was because they had to go through three or four doorways together, which provoked battles over precedence. Another tense time was when she had visitors: her paying attention to someone

else seemed to set them off. Armed with these observations, Mrs Scott was able to set up a regime which
avoided fights altogether. She payed as little attention to
the dogs as possible, took them out walking separately
and shut them in another room when friends called.

Obviously as a permanent regime this would have been
intolerable, but as a temporary measure it enabled her to
go on to systematic desensitization. This is the treatment
method for phobias described in Chapter 5, but it can be
useful for treating any kind of behaviour problem where
an identifiable stimulus provokes arousal of some kind,
whether it be aggression, fear or excitement. The principle
is the same as in the treatment of phobias. The stimulus
which provokes the arousal is presented to the dog in a
mild form, while he is doing something, like relaxing or
eating, which is incompatible with aggression, excitement
or whatever. The intensity of the stimulus is then gradually
increased. I suggested that Mrs Scott should tackle the
doorway problem by taking the dogs through the doorway in a fixed order: Spot first and then Smudge. Each
dog was to be rewarded with a delicious tit-bit if he
went through the door without looking round for the
other and growling. She was to start taking them through
the door with a thirty-second interval between them.
Then she was to bring them through the door gradually
closer and closer together, still keeping them in the
same order of precedence. (She was also to take steps to
sort out the dominance hierarchy in the household: see
Chapter 9.)

This method of treatment is usually successful if it is
carried out properly. But it can be difficult to devise a
set of stimuli suitably graded from mild to strong. How
do you stage a mild thunder clap for a dog who is afraid
of thunderstorms? How do you stage a mild version of
the owner leaving the house: surely either he goes out
or he doesn't? In the case of noises, like thunder, a tape
recorder can be useful. You can then turn on and off

the stimulus at will and you can vary the volume level. In cases like the departure of the owner, the answer is often to break the event down into its components. Often dogs who are upset when they are left alone get more and more worked up as the owner goes through his habitual pre-departure routine – collecting car keys, putting on his coat, etc. It may be comparatively easy to get the dog to stay calm while the owner does each of these things separately.

An accomplice is often essential to desensitization. If you want to desensitize your dog to the sound of someone approaching the house and ringing the bell, you might start off by desensitizing him to the sound of the latch on the gate being lifted, without the more provoking sound of footsteps coming up the path. This would happen only rarely in the normal course of events. Also, you need it to happen at the same time as the dog is performing the response incompatible with anxiety: perhaps when he is sitting beside you eating a tit-bit. The only way to bring this about is to enlist someone else's help in the training sessions.

Systematic desensitization often needs a great deal of time and patience. It may also call for some odd behaviour in public places, which deters some owners from carrying it out.

> Bessie, the bearded collie from Chapter 5, was being desensitized to going out for walks on a lead. After a week of keeping her in, she was so desperate for an outing that she allowed Miss Bremner to put her lead on and, eventually, to take her round the block. She refused to go out with any other member of the family, however. The solution was for another family member to accompany Bessie and Miss Bremner on the walk. Her mother did this and eventually Bessie was happy for Mrs Bremner to take hold of her lead, with Miss Bremner walking alongside. Miss Bremner gradually moved ahead of the pair, until, some days later, she could walk so far ahead that part of the time she

was out of sight round the corner. In the end, Bessie would go out with Mrs Bremner, without seeing Miss Bremner on the walk at all, as long as Miss Bremner left the house first. Miss Bremner could hide round the side of the house and then go back inside once Bessie and Mrs Bremner had left. The next step was obviously for Miss Bremner's brother to do the same as his mother had done; but when they suggested it, he refused, because he was not going to be seen by the neighbours taking part in this odd procession.

Miss Fowler was a retired school-teacher. Her red setter, Freddy, embarrassed her by barking in excitement when visitors arrived and jumping up on them. I suggested that she find someone to help her with the treatment and she approached a neighbour, Mr Young, also recently retired and extremely obliging. Mr Young's role was to be a minimally exciting visitor, in whose presence Freddy was to be taught to sit calmly. On the next visit Miss Fowler reported things were no better. I discovered that Mr Young had not only been rushing forward to greet Freddy with arms outstretched, but that this meeting had been taking place at the front door. A dog is often much calmer if he greets visitors once they have come in and sat down and I had suggested that she and Mr Young try this with Freddy. When I asked her why she had not done this, she said she could not possibly invite Mr Young inside and shut the door, because of what Mrs Young would think.

Eventually we worked out another plan which involved a female cousin, who could be invited in and had the added advantage that she ignored the dog when told to. Miss Fowler made some progress with this new helper, but the last time I saw her, the treatment was still being impeded by Mr Young. Ever obliging, he would turn up every day on the doorstep, to see his friend Freddy, and work him up to a state of high excitement. Miss Fowler felt she could not ask him to stay away for fear of hurting his feelings.

Response interruption
Sometimes it is impossible to prevent the problem behaviour, because you cannot anticipate it. Think carefully

before deciding that your dog's behaviour falls into this category, however, as it makes it much more difficult to deal with. Many owners who begin by thinking that they cannot anticipate and prevent the problem at all find when they observe the dog's behaviour more closely that they can.

If your dog's behaviour is genuinely unpreventable, you will have to do the next best thing, which is nip it in the bud. For example, some dogs run to the window barking furiously every time they hear someone pass in the street. Most will stop much more readily if you intervene when they first hear the noise, before they get locked into the excitement of barking. You may only have to call the dog; you may need to take hold of him and close his muzzle with your hand. Whatever you do, you must make sure that your intervention actually stops the barking: a failed intervention is worse than none at all. Then you must give the dog something else to do, which is rewarded: it might be coming with you into the kitchen for a biscuit, for example.

Other Treatment Methods

If you have a problem dog, other treatment methods besides psychological ones have probably been suggested to you. Here are some of the more popular ones:

Castration
Many problems are more common in male dogs than in bitches: for example, attacking people, fighting with other dogs and sexual mounting of people. Male hormones are a factor in all these kinds of behaviour: it might seem logical, therefore, to treat them by removing the source of the hormones. Unfortunately, research has shown that for most of these problems castration has only a fifty to sixty per cent chance of success. This is probably because the hormones which do the damage are circulating in the

puppy's bloodstream soon after birth and permanently alter his brain at that time. In cases where the problem is directly sexual (for example mounting or roaming away from home in search of bitches), castration has a better chance of success: around eighty to ninety per cent. Also, in a questionnaire study of fifty-eight owners who had had their dogs castrated, I found that only three considered that it had had an adverse effect on the dog. So it is worth considering castration for problems of aggression. There are also synthetic hormones (e.g. delimadinone) which can be given as an injection: these mimic the effect of castration. This enables its probable effect to be predicted, before undertaking an irreversible surgical procedure. Your vet will, of course, advise you about this.

Spaying

Most owners have their bitches spayed for reasons of convenience. Also, if it is done early enough, the operation can substantially reduce the risk of mammary tumours (breast cancer). But in some cases its aim is to improve behaviour. Unfortunately, there is no clear evidence that it has this effect.

Many owners who have consulted me about their bitches' aggression have commented that it got worse after spaying. But it was possible that there was no causal connection. For example, the bitches might have got more aggressive anyway, as they got older. To find out whether spaying really does make bitches more aggressive, another psychologist, Erica Peachey, and I carried out a survey of 300 bitches. Of these, 150 were spayed. We interviewed their owners twice: at the time of the operation and again six months later. We asked them about all aspects of their dogs' behaviour. To check on the possibility that any changes which occurred over the six months might be due to the dogs getting older rather than to the operation, we also interviewed 150 owners of bitches who were not spayed, again twice, with the same time interval. These bitches were matched with the spayed bitches in terms of age and breed.

We found that some behaviour changed in both groups. For example, both groups urinated and defecated in the house significantly less after six months; as one might expect, this change occurred most often in puppies under a year old. The only significant difference between the two groups was in the change in dominance aggression towards the family. The main difference was in the bitches who were showing some aggression already. In the spayed group, forty per cent of these got worse after spaying and fifty per cent improved. In the unspayed group, over the six months, seventy per cent improved and only twenty per cent got worse. The practical implication of this seems to be that if your bitch is showing signs of dominance towards you, it might be better not to have her spayed unless there is a medical reason for it: the aggression is more likely to improve if you leave her alone.

Getting another dog
You may wonder whether getting another dog would help. It seldom does. At best it adds further complications to the domestic routine. At worst it exacerbates the first dog's problem: for example, if he sees himself as pack leader in the household, having another dog to boss about is likely to make him even more dominant. You might even end up with two problem dogs: sometimes the owner of a dog who chews things up when he is left on his own gets another dog to keep him company; the result is often two dogs who chew things up.

Changing the diet
Owners of problem dogs often wonder if they should feed the dog on something different. It has been suggested by Roger Mugford, an animal behaviourist, that some problems of aggression are due to the dog's inability to

metabolize certain by-products in some processed dog foods. He has found that these cases improve on a diet of lamb and rice. There is also some evidence that animals who are hyperactive or excitable are calmer when fed on less protein and more carbohydrate. Although there is no conclusive evidence on these points, there is no harm in experimenting with dietary changes, providing you do so in consultation with your vet.

Drugs
Many owners hope for a pill to make their dogs behave better. There are drugs which can be helpful in some dog problems: perhaps the most commonly used is megestrol, a synthetic hormone which can reduce aggression and may also act as a tranquillizer. They should be used only as an aid to treatment, however. For a problem to be cured, a dog must learn new ways of behaving and new ways of viewing the world. A drug cannot teach him that. It can only, in certain cases, help to put him in the mood to learn. Another drawback of some drugs, such as megestrol, is that they cannot be given continuously for more than a matter of weeks, without risk of side-effects.

Having said that, there are occasions when drugs can be useful, especially in a crisis. Your vet can prescribe them and you should consult him if you think they might be helpful. Their use for particular problems is discussed in Chapters 9, 10 and 11.

Assessing Treatment Progress

You should review the progress of treatment every week or so. This should be done as formally as you can bear to, with all the family present. If no change has taken place in the dog's behaviour over the week, or he has got worse, then you should rethink your treatment strategy. It may not need to be altered radically: sometimes changing the timing of a reward by a few seconds can make all the difference. If some change has taken place, however slight, you should continue on the same lines.

If Treatment Fails

With the best will in the world, it sometimes turns out to be impossible to change a dog's behaviour enough to make him tolerable to live with. The agonizing question then arises of what to do with him. Unfortunately, most problems tend to persist even with new owners. For this reason it is unfair to both dog and prospective owner to take him to an animal shelter, where a new owner might take him on with no knowledge of what to expect.

If you are determined to re-home a problem dog, it is much better to find a new owner yourself. You should be absolutely honest about the difficulties you have had. You should not let the dog go to the new owner unless you are satisfied that there is a positive reason why he can deal with the problem better than you can: for example, a dog who was unreliable with children might be alright with a childless couple. A pedigree dog has a better chance of finding a satisfactory new home than a mongrel: you can make use of the rescue service run by most breed societies. Many behaviour problems are typical of a breed and, if you are lucky, you may find an enthusiast who is not bothered by your dog's behaviour and in fact has ten others who show it in varying degrees.

Unfortunately, in many cases such a happy solution is not possible. Dogs who attack without warning or destroy the house in the owner's absence cannot be blamed for what they do, but they cannot be tolerated in any household either. Euthanasia is the only possible course of action. It is always heart-breaking when this happens, but you should take some comfort from the fact that you have been a caring and responsible owner. If you have tried to put the problem right and failed, you have done your best, you have looked after your dog right to the end, you have ensured that his death is painless and you have not consigned him to an uncertain future.

9 • *Problems of Aggression*

Biting is one of the habits which give dogs a bad name. The anti-dog lobby is quick to seize on stories of dogs who maul sheep or kill babies. Unfortunately, these pressure groups are correct when they insist that aggression is a serious problem in dogs. In my survey of dog-owners I found that sixteen per cent had dogs who were in the habit of biting visitors or members of the household.

In a sense, society has only itself to blame for dogs who bite. As was discussed in Chapter 4, aggression is a natural instinct in dogs. But, as with any other instinctive behaviour, it is possible to reduce it by selective breeding. The trouble is that the dog-buying public want to have their cake and eat it. They want dogs who will defend them against the unwelcome attentions of burglars and muggers but who will not attack their friends or the man who comes to mend the washing machine. It is possible to own a ferocious dog who only attacks with your approval, but handling such a dog is a specialist skill.

A dog who barks when strangers approach the house – even if it is an excited rather than a menacing bark – is enough to deter most burglars. If you are an ordinary owner, you should content yourself with that degree of protection and never encourage a dog to threaten or attack anyone: you may end up with a situation you cannot handle. Also, unless you know what you are doing, you are best to avoid breeds which are specifically bred as guard dogs.

Mr Nicholson came to consult me about Nero, a
Rhodesian ridgeback. Nero was a magnificent dog, but
huge: the size of a small pony. Mr Nicholson was
dressed in a smart leather jacket and had heavy gold
rings on his fingers. He ran a 'business', the nature
of which was never specified, and he had bought Nero
to guard the premises. Encouraged by Mr Nicholson,
Nero did this very efficiently. If anyone came in when
Mr Nicholson was not there, he would rush up to
them growling and snarling. The trouble was that he
interpreted his job description too literally. On one
occasion Mr Nicholson and his nephew were leaving the
building together. At the doorway the nephew turned,
said 'Hang on, I've forgotten my jacket', and before Mr
Nicholson could stop him, went back into the office.
Mr Nicholson raced after him and found him pinned
to the floor, with Nero's paws on his chest and Nero
growling in his face.

But owners can be held directly responsible for their
dogs' aggression in only a minority of cases. In any case,
attributing blame is a fruitless exercise. If you own a biting
dog, you need to know what to do about it. The first step
is diagnosis: what kind of aggression is your dog showing?

Diagnosis: Predatory versus Dominance Aggression

In predatory aggression, the dog's aim is to maim or kill.
It is part of the sequence of actions aimed at getting
food. Dominance aggression is a social message directed
at creatures the dog perceives as belonging to the same
species as himself: as being dogs. Its aim is to persuade
the victim to submit.

If your dog chases cats or sheep, this is almost certain to
be predatory aggression. Chasing cars and bicycles is also
predatory aggression. Usually dogs do not try to attack
these machines, but this is probably because, viewed at
close quarters, they present an anatomical puzzle.

When dogs attack other dogs, this is usually dominance

aggression. The exceptions, however, can be dangerous. In dogs such as greyhounds, the urge to chase prey is very strong. This urge may even be triggered by the sight of small running dogs. The small dog, if caught, will probably roll over in submission, but the greyhound will continue to attack, because he does not regard his victim as another dog. Owners walking small dogs should be careful if they meet a greyhound off the lead.

In the same way, most attacks on human beings are dominance aggression, but there are exceptions. Joggers can stimulate predatory aggression. Although it usually amounts to no more than a bit of barking and chasing, it can be embarrassing. Much more seriously, dogs occasionally attack babies. If they have not been introduced to babies early in life, they may not realize that they are human and may regard them as legitimate prey. Predatory aggression is particularly likely to be stimulated by sound and movement: even if the dog is unconcerned by the sight of a baby in a pram, it is not safe to assume that it is all right to leave him alone with the baby gurgling and kicking on a rug, until you have observed his reaction. The breeds which seem to be most dangerous from this point of view are the terriers, presumably because they were originally bred to hunt and kill small prey such as rats.

It should be emphasized that these attacks are very rare, but of course every one is a tragedy. There have been instances in the USA of dogs carrying out predatory attacks on children or old people. An elderly lady, living with her son, was killed by his five mongrels when he was out. They were small dogs, but an animal behaviourist trying to reconstruct the situation found that she could rouse them to a frenzy by screaming and waving her arms about.

There is no doubt that dogs are more prone to predatory aggression when they are in groups: they can become like a pack of hunting wolves. But packs of stray dogs roaming the streets are usually less menacing than they look. If you feel alarmed, remember that they are unlikely to attack if you keep still and quiet.

Treatment of predatory aggression
Predatory aggression presents a problem of different degrees, depending on what animal is being attacked. Owners often feel that hunting rabbits or squirrels is a harmless recreation, especially if the dog does not catch any. At the other end of the spectrum, dogs who attack children or babies cannot, of course, be tolerated. Dogs who attack cats, bicycles and sheep lie somewhere between these extremes.

Predatory aggression is difficult to treat, which means that prevention is particularly important. Puppies should not be encouraged to chase any animals. They should be actively discouraged from chasing cats or sheep by being shown these creatures early in life, while being rewarded for staying calm and well behaved in their presence.

If a dog once develops an interest in chasing something, it is extremely difficult to make the object of that interest neutral and boring. The best hope of keeping the problem manageable is usually to increase your degree of general control over the dog, so that there is more chance of his obeying when you tell him to abandon a chase. If you own a hunter and chaser, you will probably have discovered already that the earlier you intervene, the better your chance of success. If you say 'No' as soon as he catches sight of the cat, sheep or whatever, he is more likely to pay attention than if he is a dot on the horizon. It may seem rather like the White Queen in *Alice Through the Looking Glass* who cried before the brooch pricked her, but you have an even better chance of success if you say 'No' before he has even seen his prey. This is because the prohibition is an assertion of dominance on your part. Dogs whose predatory aggression is a problem are often too dominant in the household. There are many dogs who would like to chase things, but refrain because their owners forbid them. It is often worth reducing the dominance of predatory aggressors as described later in this chapter.

Also, to increase your degree of control in the specific danger situation, you should practise calling the dog to you, rewarding him, maybe with a tit-bit, when he comes. Begin by doing this at quiet times and places when there is nothing to distract him: do not let him stray far before you call him. Then gradually increase the distance between you; also the degree of distraction and provocation he is exposed to. This is a kind of systematic desensitization. Instead of learning to stay calm in the presence of an exciting stimulus, he is learning to come to you. Try to avoid situations where he would be exposed to intolerable temptation, until you think you have sufficient control over him. If he does run off after something, do not call unless or until you think there is a reasonable chance he will obey. Every time you call and he ignores you, he has had another lesson in disobedience. And of course never punish him when he does eventually come back, whatever crimes he has committed. (If you do not see why not, read Chapter 3.)

You may have heard stories like the one about the dog whose owner cured him of chasing cars by hiding up a tree with buckets of water. Whenever a car passed she poured one over him. These stories always seem to be about the friend of a friend; I myself have never met anyone who has personally succeeded with this kind of strategy. As we saw in Chapter 3, punishment is a treatment method fraught with pitfalls: I suspect that for every dog cured by buckets of water, there are ten who have been unaffected, got worse or have developed a phobia of some irrelevant stimulus such as the pavement.

However, if the situation is a desperate one, punishment is worth a try. There are some dogs who become so obsessed with sheep chasing that they spend their waking moments trying to sneak out of the house and off to the sheep field. I have heard of such cases being successfully treated with a shock collar, but again I have never met one personally. It is also worth bearing in mind that many of these dogs make perfectly acceptable pets in an urban environment; this is one of the few instances where finding another home may be a satisfactory solution.

Dominance Aggression Directed against People

Dominance aggression is the commonest of the serious behaviour problems. It also aggravates many more problems which, on the face of it, are quite unrelated.

Aggression directed against the owner
In these cases the dog feels he is the pack leader and that his owner is one of his subordinates. When he thinks his subordinate is challenging the dominance, he puts him in his place by growling at him and, if necessary, biting. This was what happened in the case of William, the cairn terrier in Chapter 4 who bit Mr Watson when he was watching television. The same issue was at the root of the problem with Jasper.

> Jasper was a five-year-old black Labrador. His middle-aged owner, Mrs Jeffrey, told me that the problem was that he sniffed visitors, as she put it, 'everywhere'. If she or her husband tried to pull him off, he would turn on them, growling and snapping. Another problem was that he had taken possession of a chair in the sitting-room. One day, when cleaning out his basket, Mrs Jeffrey had thrown the rug from it over the chair and ever since he had regarded it as his exclusive property. Anyone who came near was growled at. He had taken a particular dislike to the daughter of the house. Whenever she came in, he growled at her and snapped if she tried to pat him. He also had another irritating habit. About 3 am he would start to bark, until someone got up and went through to him. He did not seem to want anything particular: as soon as he saw them he would go back to his chair and settle down again.

Jasper reacted with aggression to actions he perceived as threats to his dominance: trying to stop him doing something, invading his special territory (in this case his bed) and patting him. It seems to be the gesture of stretching out an arm above the dog which is the threatening thing about patting. Different dogs seem to feel threatened by different things. Some may take offence if someone comes near them when they are eating or if someone tries to groom them.

Causes and treatment
As mentioned in Chapter 4, dogs of certain breeds (for example guard dogs and terriers) are more prone to dominance aggression. This information is not much use if you already own one. On the other hand, we know that it is more common in male dogs and this fact is potentially more useful: castration helps in about fifty per cent of cases. To find out if you are one of the lucky ones, your vet can first give your dog an injection of delmadinone, a drug which has the same effect as castration.

In a crisis, however, or if your dog has really got the upper hand, the drug megestrol is likely to be of more immediate help. This is a synthetic female hormone, a progestagen, which is given to bitches to stop them coming into season. It also makes many dogs more amenable and easier to dominate. Because of the risk of undesirable side-effects, it should be given to dogs (castrated or otherwise) and spayed bitches for no longer than two or three weeks at the full dose. After that the dose should be gradually tapered off over another two weeks. Bitches who have not been spayed should have it for no longer than a week. The drug does not, by itself, make a dog less dominant. It provides a window of opportunity for the owner to establish a new relationship over him.

Whatever may be the other factors which cause a dog to be dominant, the owner's role is crucial. In order for a dog to be dominant, an owner must allow himself to be dominated. There are two main ways this can happen. As was seen in Chapter 4, it can come about if an owner permits his dog always to take the social initiative.

> Mr and Mrs Taylor were a cheerful couple in their fifties. They were very fond of Terry, an attractive young golden Labrador. Mrs Taylor's mother, who lived with them, absolutely doted on him. Terry had never been aggressive to any human being, but it was clear that his dominance over the Taylors played a key part in his problem. When he was let off the lead on a walk, he would make a bee-line for any other dog, growling and snarling. If Mr Taylor called him to come back, he paid not the slightest attention. Mrs Taylor had long ago refused to take him out, because of the embarrassment involved. Mr Taylor had tried obedience classes, but had felt forced to abandon them, because the trainer kept warning the other members of the class to 'mind the yellow dog'.
> Terry obviously played a central role in the Taylors' domestic social life. When Mr Taylor got up early to go to work, Terry would bounce up and down in front of him 'on all four feet', until he was taken for a walk: 'not a long one, only 100 yards, but until he has it, he won't let me alone'. Then, throughout the day, he made his wishes known to Mrs Taylor and her mother. If he wanted a biscuit, he went to the tin and barked. If he was thirsty, he put his paws up on the sink until someone turned the tap on. His evening walk was preceded by an elaborate ritual. He would first of all go to Mrs Taylor as she sat in her chair and he would bark. She would say, 'Do you want me to tell him?' Terry would bark again, whereupon Mrs Taylor would say, 'John, it's time for his walk'. Terry would then move in front of John's chair, where he would bounce up and down until Mr Taylor got up to fetch his lead.

Terry was a charming dog and the Taylors fell in with his wishes because they enjoyed it: they did not feel bullied at all. Their family had grown up and left home; Terry filled a gap in their lives very neatly. Unfortunately, because of Terry's dominant temperament, he construed the situation differently. The purpose of many of his requests was not to get food, water or whatever: sometimes, when he was given biscuits, he did not even eat them. Their purpose was to confirm his dominance. (Incidentally, Jasper was probably doing a similar thing when he barked in the middle of the night. He did not want anything: he was simply forcing someone to respond.)

If the owner constantly backs down in confrontations, this can encourage the dog to think he is dominant. Owners are usually aware this is happening when they ask the dog to do something and he refuses. But it can also happen in situations which the dog construes as serious confrontations, but the owner does not: playing tug-of-war games, for example.

> A young couple, Mr and Mrs Eastwood, told me about another, more peculiar way in which they were encouraging their dog's dominance. Egbert, their Old English sheepdog, was becoming difficult at the end of car journeys. When they opened the tail-gate of their hatchback, he growled and refused to come out. When I asked about their domestic routine with him, a curious ritual came to light. Mr Eastwood was concerned about Egbert's poor appetite. To coax the dog into eating breakfast, he would prepare a plate of cornflakes and milk for himself, put it on the floor, take up his spoon and start to eat. Egbert would then rush forward and start to eat too, pushing Mr Eastwood out of the way. Mr Eastwood would withdraw, satisfied that he had achieved his object. Egbert probably saw the situation quite differently: he probably felt that he had successfully asserted his dominance over his owner and his superior right to the cornflakes.

Sometimes dogs become dominant not because their owners comply with their demands, but because their owners leave them on their own too much.

> Mrs Russell was a bright, brittle young woman, perhaps best described as a Morningside yuppie. She had two young children and two Cavalier King Charles

spaniels, Rowley and Rona. They were not show dogs,
but, unusually, they were both in full possession of
their reproductive organs and had produced three litters between them. The trouble had started when the
Russells' upward mobility had moved them from a flat
into a house with a garden. In the flat, the dogs
had lived mostly in the kitchen. When they moved, it
seemed to Mrs Russell a good idea to give them a
basement room all to themselves from which they could
have free access, via a cat door, to the garden. It was
then that the problems started. Rowley and the children
had always enjoyed playing together, but now, when
they played in the garden, Rowley would suddenly take
the game too seriously. He would decide that he wanted
sole possession of the ball and would growl at anyone who suggested someone else should have a turn.
Eventually he leapt up at one boy who tried to take the
ball away and bit him on the nose. At this point Mrs
Russell saw that something would have to be done.

What had happened was that once Rowley had been
allotted his own territory, he began to regard himself and
Rona as a separate pack, with himself as leader. When
anyone visited his territory, which included the garden,
he felt he had a right to dictate what they did there.

If you are being dominated by your dog, how should you
go about establishing yourself as leader? To some extent,
your strategy will depend on how your dog's dominance
came about. If you have been, like Mr and Mrs Taylor, a
friendly and obliging owner who has allowed your dog to
take all the social initiatives, then you should proceed as
follows:

Ignore your dog for long stretches of time. Do not chat
to him about the state of the nation or ask his opinion on
whether it will rain this afternoon. Even more important, if
he comes up to you and asks for something, whether it is a
cuddle or a pat or to be let out into the garden, ignore him
(Fig. 12). This behaviour of yours will have two effects: it
will make your attention a rare and valuable commodity.
He will be more prepared to work hard to get it. Also, it

Fig. 12
Asserting dominance over a dog
by ignoring his demands.

will convey to him the message that you are dominant. Be particularly strict about not paying him attention if he jumps on to your knee or puts his paws on it. These are dominant postures for a dog: they should be discouraged by getting up and walking away or by pushing him off without making eye contact. If you find all this difficult to do, that is a hopeful sign: it means there is a lot of room for improvement. If, when you start behaving in this stand-offish way, the dog looks confused and depressed, this is also a hopeful sign: he is in the process of changing his view of the world.

The next step is to use your attention and other rewards (e.g. having a ball thrown, being let into the garden) to reinforce submissive behaviour, in other words obedience to your commands. For example, having ignored him when he whined and pawed at the door to get out, a few minutes later, when he has given up, you should call him; tell him to sit and, when he does so, open the door to let him out. 'Lie down' is another good command to use in this context, because lying down is itself a submissive posture.

It is important to keep up this pattern of interaction throughout the day. The aim is to arrange the dog's life so that it proceeds pleasantly only as long as he behaves in a submissive way. It is also worth practising obedience drill ('Sit', 'Stay', etc.) for a ten-minute session every day, for two reasons. Firstly, in this situation, you are firmly in the dominant role: because of this, all adult members of the household should practise with the dog. Secondly, the better he is conditioned in training sessions to respond automatically to a command, the greater the likelihood he will do so in real life when it matters.

If, on the other hand, your dog has become dominant because he has been on his own too much, your strategy should contain an additional element. As well as ignoring his demands, you should, as far as possible, be in control of his waking life. Do not let him wander off on his own, but keep him under your command, telling him to sit and stay, come with you, etc. This may mean modifying his routine, so that he comes with you when you go out, even if he has to stay in the car most of the time; he might also sleep in your bedroom rather than in the kitchen.

After a week or two, you should begin to sense a change in your relationship. Until this happens, as far as possible avoid entering into aggressive confrontations with the dog. The best way of doing this is to rearrange his life so that there is no chance of these confrontations arising. For example, Jasper growled if he was disturbed on his chair. I suggested that this chair should be taken out of the room so that he had no chance to sit on it in the first place. Similarly, with Egbert, the Old English sheepdog who growled when his owners tried to get him out of the car, I suggested that until they had become more dominant over him they should not take him out in the car at all. An extension of this principle is that owners should not give an order unless they think the dog is likely to obey it. Every time a dog disobeys a command, he is behaving in a dominant way.

Once the owners sense that they have become more dominant over the dog, they should gradually reintroduce the problematic situations. This is a form of systematic desensitization: the emotion to be unlearnt is not fear but aggression; the state of mind which inhibits it is not relaxation but being subordinate. Suppose, for example, that your dog growls and snaps when you try to groom him, especially when you try to comb his ears. You should first of all plan a week or two when you will not groom him at all. If he is a long-haired dog it can be helpful to have his coat cut short. It takes courage to be seen in public with a Pekinese with short hair, but it can be well worth it. When you feel you have become more dominant over him, carry out a series of training sessions which start by your emphasizing your dominance over him: perhaps by telling him to sit. You may find that he is more amenable when not on his own territory: for example, when he is not in the kitchen, but in the bathroom, so start the sessions there. Then begin gradually by merely producing the hair brush and putting it away again. If he can tolerate a few sessions of this, without looking put out, you might then progress to brushing him lightly once or twice on an insensitive part of his anatomy such as his back. You should then, over a matter of a week or two, move by easy stages to the problematic ears.

Mrs Innes was an elderly widow who lived in the flat below her son and his family. When she thought of getting a dog to keep her company, her son had persuaded her to get a bearded collie. He had, in fact, chosen the puppy for her: she was called Irene. Now a year old, she was friendly and enchanting to all visitors: the grandchildren adored her and came down regularly after school to fuss over her and give her sweets. Mrs Innes's son took her out for long walks at weekends. Mrs Innes was very fond of her, too, but there were problems. When she was let out in the garden to 'do her business' she would not come in when Mrs Innes called: this was all right in the summer, when Mrs Innes left the door open and she wandered in and out at will. But in the winter, Irene, having studiously ignored Mrs Innes's call, would sit outside the kitchen door, whining pathetically. If Mrs Innes opened the door, she would either wander away again or sit in the doorway, half in, half out, so that Mrs Innes could not shut it. Much more alarmingly, when she and Mrs Innes were alone in the house, if Mrs Innes sneezed, Irene would spring at her, growling and snarling.

The basic trouble with Irene was, of course, that she had come to be dominant over Mrs Innes. When Mrs Innes sneezed, Irene felt this as a threat (perhaps it sounded a bit like a growl) and reacted accordingly. Underlying Irene's performance in the garden was the principle that she must take all the social initiatives.

To treat the problem, I suggested first of all that Mrs Innes set about establishing dominance over Irene by the recommended method: by ignoring her demands and rewarding obedience. Irene, who had been spayed, was put on a course of megestrol. We worked out the following strategy for the sneezing problem: whenever Mrs Innes felt a sneeze coming on, she would quickly shut herself in another room away from Irene. While we were discussing the matter, Mrs Innes had tried deliberately making various sneezing noises; we found that the more realistic they were, the more violently Irene reacted. So Mrs Innes was to systematically desensitize Irene by telling her to sit and then making a sneezing noise, starting with a token snort and gradually working up to a full-blown sneeze.

The plan for tackling the problem about the garden was that when Irene went out, Mrs Innes was to leave her for a long time, until she was desperate to come back inside. Mrs Innes was to ignore all pathetic faces at the door. Eventually, Mrs Innes was to open the door, pretend she was not waiting for Irene to come in, but when she saw Irene coming in, she was to call her. The rationale of this plan was that to begin with, when Irene stayed out in the garden, she would never do so in defiance of Mrs Innes. When she came in she would always be 'obeying' a command of Mrs Innes. Eventually Mrs Innes would find that she could give an effective real command: one which preceded the action.

In books about psychological problems, be they human or animal, you can tell the case histories that are made up by the fact that when the patient does as the psychologist tells him, he always gets better. When he is naughty and does not follow the instructions, he is, as in any good fairy story, punished: usually by getting worse. Life, of course, is not like that. And effective psychological treatment does not consist of a set of magic instructions. When I see a client, my aim is to discuss the possible causes of the problem and the psychological principles underlying treatment. Although I make suggestions as to how it might be done, it is up to the clients to apply these principles in their own lives.

Mrs Innes was a good example of this. As a result of our discussion, she decided that the main problem was that she was not in sole charge of Irene. So, from then on, she made clear to her son and his family that they were all to obey her orders as regards Irene. The grandchildren were not allowed to make a fuss of her and certainly not allowed to give her sweets. She also stopped worrying about Irene catching cold in the garden (an unfounded worry given the thickness of a bearded collie's coat): she took the attitude that if Irene wanted to stay there she could stew in her own juice. As for the sneezing problem, she found a new commanding tone of voice which did the trick. If she felt a sneeze coming on, she would say to Irene 'Down' in this new voice: Irene might rumble a bit in her throat but did not attack.

What seems to have happened in this case was that Mrs Innes saw her relationship with Irene from a different perspective. This led to subtle changes in her behaviour towards Irene: she was probably not even aware of many of them. Also the megestrol may have made Irene more receptive towards the change in Mrs Innes: more ready to accept her new subordinate role gracefully. The result was that matters resolved quickly without having to resort to the fine print of the treatment instructions.

Variants of Dominance Aggression

Aggression towards strangers
Sometimes the dog's aggression is directed not at the owners, but at people outside the family. Like Nero, they may attack visitors to the house. They may attack people in the street, especially those who stop to speak to the owner.

The dog's dominance over the owner lies at the root of these problems as well: he is behaving like a pack leader, defending the pack's territory or other pack members. The treatment strategy should be similar, too. The owner should set about establishing dominance over the dog and then systematically desensitize him to the situations which provoke the aggression. For a dog who threatens visitors, the systematic desensitization might go like this:
1. When ordinary visitors call, shut the dog away in another room.
2. Arrange for an accomplice to call. This should be someone who is likely to provoke only a slight amount of aggression in the dog: maybe a female friend of the family.
3. Territorial aggression is often worse if the dog is allowed to meet the visitor at the door. If this is the case, try shutting the dog away until the visitor is inside and

sitting down: then bring him in to meet her, under your command.

4. If this is successful, arrange meetings with other accomplices in the same circumstances: these 'visitors' should be progressively more threatening from the dog's point of view, perhaps men or people who are less well known.

5. The next step is to move the meeting place to the door. When the bell rings, have the dog sit beside you under your command, before you open it.

As with straightforward dominance aggression, a course of megestrol may be helpful.

Fear biting

There is a kind of aggression which is sometimes called 'fear biting'. Before he bites, the dog crouches down, with ears back, as if in fear. A variant, common in border collies, is that when strangers try to pat him, the dog cowers, but when they turn away, he gives them a disconcerting nip on the back of the leg. These dogs are often more dangerous than straightforwardly aggressive dogs, because it can be more difficult to predict what they are going to do. Otherwise, the problem should be treated in exactly the same way as simple dominance aggression: the systematic desensitization will deal with the fear element of the dog's reaction as well as with the aggressive element.

Rage syndrome

This is a variant of dominance aggression which has been particularly common in whole-colour cocker spaniels lately, though it can occur in other breeds. The dog attacks suddenly and savagely, without preliminary threats. Because the victim has no warning and no chance to move away, the result is often a flesh wound which needs medical treatment. During the attack the dog often has a glazed look: he does not seem to be in touch with his surroundings.

This kind of behaviour has been classified by some experts as a separate syndrome: maybe as some kind of illness like epilepsy. But in the cases I have seen, the dog is simply showing a dangerous form of dominance aggression, in which he moves from threat to attack very quickly. Owners may feel that the dog's attack on them is completely unprovoked, but I have found that the owner always does something, even though it may be trivial, which the dog might construe as a threat to his dominance.

> A golden cocker called Sammy, owned by Mrs Sanderson, was liable to bite his owner if she brushed against him, particularly if he was near the refrigerator: he was in the habit of hovering around when she opened its door in the hope of scraps.

In my experience, these cases respond to the standard treatment for dominance aggression. Having said that, I have also found that, on the whole, their prognosis is not good, because in order for treatment to be successful the attacks must be eliminated entirely. If the dog backslides even once, he is unlikely to be given a second chance.

Mrs Sanderson was very fond of Sammy and worked hard at his treatment. She achieved significant success, too. Though Sammy sometimes growled at her, he never bit her again. Unfortunately the whole thing came unstuck at Christmas (a risky time for family relationships in general and dog behaviour problems in particular – I always have a spate of referrals at the beginning of January). Mrs Sanderson's mother-in-law was staying with them and on Christmas Eve was helping Mrs Sanderson wrap presents at the foot of the tree. Sammy was helping too and the mother-in-law's arm happened to brush against his back legs. He turned and bit her; there was a terrible scene: blood all over the carpet and presents, mother-in-law hysterical, Mr Sanderson, who had never liked Sammy, beside himself with rage. Mrs Sanderson had to bow to majority opinion and Sammy was taken then and there to the vet to be destroyed.

Dominance without aggression

As mentioned in Chapter 8, dominance issues may underly some problems in which the dog shows no aggression at all. Dogs who obey owners' commands only when it suits them may not feel their owners are authorized to order them around. If you are not sure whether your dog sees himself as your subordinate or not, reflect on his general life-style. Dominant dogs tend to live independent lives. They may be affectionate to their owners, but only intermittently, when it suits them. When in the house with their owners, they will spontaneously wander away into a different room to sleep, look out of the window or go into the garden to explore. They often do not mind spending the night in a part of the house separate from the owner, which may give a false impression of compliance. A subordinate dog, on the other hand, typically likes to keep his owners in view most of the time: the owner is the centre of his universe.

A Treatment Method not Recommended

Owners of aggressive or disobedient dogs are often advised to stage a series of confrontations with them and to win these confrontations by violent and dramatic means. They are advised to hit them, shake them by the scruff of the neck, make them squeal, show them who's boss, etc. This scenario appeals to some people. But if you have a dog who has already managed to dominate you, you probably find it rather alarming and distasteful. Whatever your attitude, it is not a method to be recommended, for two reasons. First of all, it is too risky. If your dog sees you as a subordinate, challenging him is a good way of getting bitten. Comparative strangers may be able to challenge your dog successfully: your vet may stop him biting with a tap on the nose. But you may not be able to do the same thing safely if you are established in a subordinate relationship to him.

The second reason why direct challenges are not a good idea, even if you win them, is that they tend to raise the emotional temperature of the relationship between you and the dog and to focus attention on the issue of dominance. A series of confrontations which the dog has lost may make him keen to win back his position at the first opportunity. It is much better to undermine the dog's dominance by low-key and subtle means, like those described earlier.

This is not to say that winning a confrontation with a dog is itself a bad thing. It is obviously better for the owner to win than to lose. Also, winning can be a great boost to an owner's morale and make him feel more confident and dominant. It makes a great difference to know that, if push comes to shove, you can get the better of your dog: turn him off a chair or rescue the packet of sausages he has stolen. It is not safe to tackle a large, dominant dog head on, but you can usually get the better of a small one, if you use a pair of thick gardening gloves or grab him by the scruff of the neck.

I am not recommending that you should never hit your dog or shout at him crossly. Hitting and speaking in a fierce, growly tone of voice are dominant actions; there are times, when you want to emphasize your dominance, when they can be useful. Suppose, for example, that you have established dominance over your dog, but he suddenly tries to go for the man who has come to mend the washing machine. Shouting 'No' and hitting the dog may be the best way of stopping him: what you are saying to him, in effect, is 'Have you forgotten who's boss around here? If anyone bites the washing machine man, it's me.'

Dog Attacks Dog

Aggression between dogs can occur in two different situations: between dogs from the same household or between dogs from different households.

Fights between dogs from different households

When strange dogs meet, growling and posturing is not uncommon. In fact, without a bit of aggression, one might almost say that social life among owners using the same park would lose some of its spice. A substantial part of their conversation deals with whose dog does not get on with whose, whose dog is not to be trusted and who does not keep their dog under proper control. Having said that, it can be embarrassing to be one of the owners at whose approach everyone puts their dogs on the lead. And if your dog has had one or two serious fights, it can be downright worrying.

If your dog is one of those, the first step is to decide whether he is an aggressor or a victim. Some dogs who have left their mother and litter-mates too soon (at six weeks old or earlier) may not have had the chance to learn how to behave properly in encounters with other dogs: how to signal submission, for example, to a bigger, more aggressive dog. These dogs may constantly be victims. If you have a dog like this, you can never make up entirely for the early experience he has lost, but you may be able to compensate to some extent by arranging for him to meet and play with a wide range of friendly dogs: in this way he may be able to learn a bit more about dog social conventions.

There is no magic cure, either, for dogs who are the aggressors in fights. In some, castration may reduce the urge to fight. Megestrol can be a temporary help. Usually your best hope is to gain better control over the dog, so that he pays more attention to you when you tell him to ignore another dog. To achieve this, you will probably have to increase your dominance over him. (This is the advice I gave to Mr Taylor, whose Labrador, Terry, attacked other dogs.) It is often helpful, too, to practise in the park with your dog when there are no others around: call him to you constantly and reward him for coming. Always call him when you are pretty sure he will obey. Start by calling him when he is not far away and there are no distractions. Gradually increase your control by taking him out at busier times and letting him go further before you call him. When you actually meet another dog, call him and establish your control as early as you can: before he has even noticed the other dog or while it is still far away in the distance.

Fights between dogs from the same household
Fights are fairly frequent in multi-dog households. Usually they are playful; if they become serious it is only for a few moments. There may be an argument over a bone or the occupation of a basket; it may involve a lot of growling or even baring of teeth, but it is usually settled without any physical violence. Occasionally, however, the aggression in a household may escalate until the dogs do each other physical harm. This problem seems particularly common among the various breeds of terrier. Indeed, American psychologists Scott and Fuller found, when they were studying the psychological development of various breeds of puppy, that it was not safe to keep more than three fox terrier puppies together in the same pen. If there were four, then one puppy would hold each end of the victim and the fourth would attack the middle.

If your dogs show signs of beginning to fight in earnest, do not ignore this on the assumption that they will sort it out amongst themselves. They may well do so, but one of them may be seriously injured in the process.

Dogs in the same household usually have their own dominance hierarchy and fights are usually stirred up by ambiguities in that hierarchy, by dogs being not sure where they stand. This can happen for a number of reasons. If you get two puppies at the same time, they may happily co-exist until they mature and become more preoccupied with dominance. If they are both inclined to be dominant and are evenly matched, there may be trouble. Or a puppy may arrive in a household where there is already an adult dog. The puppy may happily accept the dominance of the older dog at first, but as he grows up, he may make a bid for leadership. Often having a litter of puppies to defend makes a bitch more dominant. Sometimes this effect persists even when the puppies have grown up and left. If the bitch was at the bottom of the hierarchy before, this may lead to ructions.

Often owners increase the dogs' confusion about dominance: in some cases the fights only take place in the owners' presence. Owners may take pains to treat each dog fairly, to give them all an equal share of attention. When the dogs fight, they often punish the aggressor, because he is the one stirring up the trouble. This is another situation where our human ideals of equality in relationships clash with a dog's assumption that a hierarchy is the natural social order. Dogs who are trying to work out which of them is dominant will be confused by being treated equally: a dog who is beginning to give up a claim to dominance may be encouraged to try again if the owners take his side.

By the same token, a change in the owner's attitude and behaviour may be highly effective in treating the problem. First of all, you should decide which dog is to be dominant. You should make this choice, not on the basis of the one you like best, but on the basis of which one is most able to maintain his position: this is often the one you like least, because he behaves in such a pushy, unpleasant way. You should then reinforce the position of this dominant dog, by giving him preference. Pay him more attention than his subordinate, feed him first, take him out leaving the other behind, and so on. If they start threatening and growling at each other, be cross with the subordinate, even if he did not start the fight and is getting the worst of it.

It is usually helpful to establish your own dominance over both dogs more firmly. This will make them feel they are both subordinates as far as the general family hierarchy is concerned. They should therefore be less preoccupied with issues of dominance: in wolf packs it is wolves near the top of the hierarchy who fight; those near the bottom live together more amicably.

Zimen observed that when there is serious fighting between two high-status wolves there is likely to be more fighting among the rest of the pack as well: it is as if uncertainty about leadership unsettles everyone. So fighting between dogs may start or get worse if there is serious conflict between human members of the household. This is particularly likely if the areas of disagreement include the dogs. Sometimes a husband and wife who are going through a difficult time in their own relationship each have their 'special dog', who is more attached to him or her. Each gives his or her own dog preference and when the dogs start fighting the couple start arguing about which dog is to blame: the dogs find this very confusing. Obviously a couple cannot settle their differences simply in order to calm the dogs down. But they may be able to take more care not to let their difficulties affect the dogs.

Sometimes, where it is appropriate, castration can be helpful, either of both dogs or of the subordinate dog. Also, megestrol given to both dogs or to the subordinate dog can help to calm a situation which is getting out of hand.

This strategy of treating the dogs differently is usually effective in sorting out conflicts of dominance, but some owners are reluctant to adopt it. They are understandably unwilling to ignore a well-established and much-loved dog, especially if this means favouring a bumptious newcomer. After all, it means not being able to enjoy the company of one of your dogs properly. In this situation, it might be best to find another home for one of the dogs in a household with no other dogs: this is one of the few situations where the re-homed dog would not take his problem with him.

10 • *Neurotic Problems*

As was seen in Chapter 5, stress and anxiety can cause a range of problems in dogs. In some cases, the anxiety or agitation is obvious; in others, it can easily be mistaken for something else, like being over-sexed or having a passion for chewing. But where an excessive state of arousal or excitement is part of the problem, it is essential to recognize and deal with it or the difficulty will never resolve.

Phobias

Isolated phobias are common in dogs: two out of three have a fear of something like the vacuum cleaner or thunderstorms. Whether your dog's phobia matters or not will depend partly on the circumstances of your life. Archie, the dog in Chapter 5 who became depressed after his companion died, developed a fear of the sound of rain on the car roof. If his domestic situation had been different, this might not have mattered very much. As it was, his owner, Miss Anderson, lived on her own and regularly had to drive long distances on business. This made Archie's symptom extremely inconvenient.

Whether a dog's phobias constitute a major problem also depends upon what he is liable to do when he is afraid. My grandmother had a cocker spaniel called Derry who in his old age developed a fear of sudden, loud noises. On one occasion, a car back-fired when they were out for a walk; he completely lost his head, dashed across a busy road and through the front door of a strange house. My grandmother dashed after him. A few minutes later, the astonished owners of the house discovered an unknown woman in their bathroom, peering under the bath and calling 'Derry, Derry, you can come out now'. Some dogs' fear drives them to destructive behaviour. I saw a golden Labrador who was afraid of thunderstorms. When a storm came on and his owners were at home he could just about cope by following them from room to room and always keeping close to them. But if they were out, he became really desperate, clawing and scraping at the doors in an effort to escape.

Systematic desensitization is an effective treatment for phobias. But it is so time-consuming that it is probably only worth contemplating if the phobia constitutes a major nuisance. The method has already been described in Chapter 5 and discussed in Chapter 8. Here is a step-by-step guide to its use for phobias:

1. Find out all the features of the stimulus which affect the degree of fear it produces. For example, in the case of fear of loud noises, these might be the intensity of the sound, its pitch, its suddenness and where it happens.

2. Using variations in these features, draw up a hierarchy of situations. Those at the bottom should produce almost no fear in the dog and those at the top should produce extreme fear. In the case of the phobia of sudden, high-pitched noises, a stimulus at the bottom of the hierarchy might be a kitchen timer going 'ping' at the bottom of the garden, whereas a stimulus at the top of the hierarchy might be a telephone ringing right next to the dog.

3. Try to arrange that over the period that the treatment is in progress, the dog is not exposed to stimuli high in the hierarchy.

4. Arrange for short, frequent treatment sessions. About ten minutes, three or four times a day, is optimum.

5. In the first treatment session, make the dog as relaxed

as possible. Talk to him soothingly, cuddle him or pat him: keep on talking to him to make sure he stays relaxed.
6. Expose him to the lowest, mildest stimulus in the hierarchy.
7. Repeat the stimulus several times, until you are sure that it arouses no anxiety in the dog.
8. Go on to the next stimulus in the hierarchy and repeat steps 5, 6 and 7.

If at any point the dog starts to show fear, it means that you are going too fast up the hierarchy. Go back a few stages. As you go up the hierarchy, you will almost certainly have to revise it to some extent. The dog will probably move through some stages more quickly than you expected; at others he may get stuck. If he does get stuck, you will have to think up more variations in the stimulus to make a more gradual set of steps at this point. For example, if a dog is not upset by the sound of a telephone ringing in the next room but is frightened by one in the same room, an intermediate stage might be achieved by muffling the telephone in the same room with a blanket.

Anxiety Neurosis

Comparatively rarely a dog may suffer from a mass of phobias, which bedevil the whole of his waking life (see the cases of Barney, Prince and Heather in Chapter 5). If you have a dog like this, the chances are that you have already consulted your vet or someone else about him. These dogs often give the whole household the jitters. Their owners may become convinced that there is something physically wrong with the dog or that they have been making terrible mistakes in their handling of him. Some of these dogs tremble so violently at routine domestic events (for example someone dropping something or someone new entering the room) or seem so out of touch with reality (for example rushing around banging into things in their fear) that they have been diagnosed as epileptic. Unless the dog also has obvious fits, where he loses consciousness completely, falls down and twitches, such a diagnosis is dubious. On the other hand, if the dog is helped by anti-epileptic drugs, well and good.

As was seen in Chapter 5, these dogs usually have inherited neurotic personalities or have had drastically abnormal experiences in early puppyhood. Very rarely are their owners responsible for their condition. Given a stable and loving home, many of these dogs improve gradually with age. However, many owners prevent this potential improvement by becoming fussed and wound up about their dog's condition. The reactions of every owner of these dogs whom I have seen have followed a similar pattern. They have tried being very respectful of the dog's feelings. The whole household has tiptoed around, under strict instructions not to make any sudden sound or movement. Visitors have been discouraged, outings elaborately planned in advance. They have often tried some form of systematic desensitization, introducing the dog gradually to the things he is afraid of. They have usually been rewarded by partial success, with some of the phobias improving, but ultimately frustration has set in as new phobias have sprung up in the place of those which have died down. Irritation often starts with this dog who makes them feel so helpless and guilty. The dog is alternately shouted at and cuddled, a regime which is not calculated to calm him down. Also, his neurotic behaviour tends to be rewarded by a lot of attention. People call to him when he cowers under a chair or try to entice him out with tit-bits. Normal behaviour may be ignored. Although this is unlikely to cause neurotic behaviour, it may prevent improvement from occurring.

I usually advise these owners that their best course of action is to resign themselves to the fact that they have a dog with a disability. They should not make strenuous efforts to try to cure him but should concentrate on working out a way of life which is tolerable both for them and for him.

They should not keep him on their minds constantly as they move around the house and they must not feel unable to have visitors or to go out. When the dog gets frightened he should just be ignored. On the other hand, he should not be forced unnecessarily to do things which terrify him. For example, he should not be forced to take walks if he hates them.

Given these more settled conditions, many of these dogs eventually improve.

Excitement in Specific Situations

Like specific fears, this is a common phenomenon; many dogs become over-excited in certain situations: Miss Hamilton's Harry got excited in the car, Mrs Boyd's Buddy when she prepared to take him for a walk. The dog may express his state of high arousal by barking or dashing to and fro. He may also perform a displacement activity (see Chapter 5): he may do something pointless and irrelevant again and again, like chasing his tail.

> Miss Liston was a school-teacher who lived with her elderly mother. When she rang me to make an appointment she said that it was 'on behalf of a little black poodle'. But when I saw them, the little black poodle, Leo, did not seem particularly eager to get help. He seemed to be enjoying himself in an over-enthusiastic sort of way, running round the consulting room, jumping up on my knee and Miss Liston's knee, all the time giving out a continuous stream of high-pitched yaps so loud and piercing that it was impossible to converse and difficult to think. Miss Liston was nearly in tears. We eventually put him in another room, where his barking was still audible through three closed doors, but muffled enough for Miss Liston to be able to tell me that at home Leo was quiet and well behaved.

It was only in a strange house that he would behave in
this way. She also told me that when Leo became
very excited he would grab her arm or her hostess's arm
with his front paws and sexually mount it; this was
clearly a displacement activity.

Poodles seem particularly prone to this kind of problem
because they are so. quick to learn. Their high-pitched,
relentless bark also seems to drive owners to distraction
very quickly. When I was carrying out my survey of
dog-owners, I stumbled across a small tragedy. I usually
approached potential subjects in the clinic waiting room,
before they saw the vet. On one occasion, I came across
a woman sitting there in tears. It turned out that she had
brought her poodle for euthanasia. The chief reason for
this decision seemed to be that he barked at the television,
especially at those advertisements for disposable nappies
in which babies dance across the screen. I explained to
her that there was a good chance that this problem could
be rectified but she was set on going ahead. When people
have already reached a decision to have a dog put down
and have come to the vet psychologically prepared for this,
it is often very difficult for them to change their minds,
especially without a one hundred per cent guarantee of
a cure.

If your dog has a problem of over-excitement, there are
two possible treatment approaches: systematic desensitization and rearrangement of rewards. In some cases,
only one of these methods will be appropriate. Others
will require a combination of the two.

Systematic desensitization
Carry out some experiments, to find out whether there
are particular situations or stimuli which set off the excitement. It may be that, like Leo, your dog responds to a wide
variety of situations. On the other hand, if you are lucky,
the stimulus which triggers maximum excitement will be
fairly specific.

Mac was an Alsatian, a police dog. He was very good
at his job and he and his handler, PC Mathieson,
competed regularly in police dog trials. He loved his
work too; he particularly enjoyed searching buildings for
criminals and arresting them by grabbing hold of their
arms. The problem arose when Mac was in the back
of the police van, cruising around between assignments.
The back of these vans were fitted out with wire-
mesh cages and as soon as Mac was put into one, he
would start to whine and bark. I asked for a demonstration and we spent half an hour driving round and
round the block in a quiet Edinburgh suburb. Mac
took up a peculiar fixed posture with his nose jammed
into the top front corner of the cage, his ears back
and a glazed look in his eyes: PC Mathieson said he
always did this. This kind of behaviour is known as a
'stereotypy'; it is often seen in zoo animals whose cages
are too small. Mac progressed from whining, through
barking on a high-pitched note, to finally trembling
and salivating profusely. PC Mathieson tried to maintain
a professional and detached calm, but by the end of
the half hour we were all a bit the worse for wear. As
well as finding the noise unbearable, PC Mathieson
was clearly very fond of his dog and was distressed to
see him in such a state. He said that in all other
situations he behaved perfectly. When he was not on
duty, Mac lived with the Mathiesons. When he travelled
in the back of PC Mathieson's private car, he was
quite calm.

The police force had taken him over as a puppy
from owners who had not been able to cope with
him: most police dogs are rescue dogs. He had been
rather too excitable initially, but PC Mathieson's training
had soon calmed him down, for the most part. He
had always been restless in the van, however, and lately
this had got much worse. PC Mathieson had tried
shouting at Mac; he had tried squirting water at him; he
had tried ignoring him: nothing seemed to make any
difference.

There seemed to be several reasons why Mac should
be over-excited when he was in the van. He was often
agitated when he went in there: for example, if hooligans

at a soccer match taunted him, he would be put into his kennel for a bit, in case matters got out of hand. Also, when Mac left the van, it was usually either to have a run in the park or to do the work he enjoyed so much. Therefore, for much of his time in the van, he was in a high state of anticipation. Added to this, there was the stress produced by confinement. I thought he was upset, too, at being separated from PC Mathieson. However, as he had managed to learn to control himself very well in other situations of stress, I thought he was probably capable of learning to be calm in this one, too.

I decided to try systematic desensitization. I suggested to PC Mathieson that he take Mac out to the van and see how he behaved if he sat on the front passenger seat. I could see that PC Mathieson was embarrassed at this prospect, but he agreed. He came back ten minutes later, saying that he had driven round the block and Mac had been as good as gold. Encouraged by this, we discussed possible ways of making a hierarchy of stimuli.

PC Mathieson started by taking the cage out of the back of the van. For a few days, Mac rode around in the back of the van, with his head on his handler's shoulder. Then he spontaneously gave that up and settled down in a more comfortable position on the floor. PC Mathieson then put up a wire-mesh barrier between the front seats and the back of the van: this separated Mac from his owner but left him the freedom of all the back of the van. He tolerated this perfectly well.

But PC Mathieson was in a hurry to make his arrangements seem more orthodox, before they attracted the adverse attention of his superiors. He went too far: it is dangerous to hurry systematic desensitization. He put up another wire-mesh barrier, at right angles to the first: this made a sort of cage. When he came for his next appointment, this had been in place for two days. Mac had clearly not liked it and had whined, though not as badly as before. PC Mathieson knew he had been rushing things; he agreed to dispense with the second barrier altogether for a while and then to introduce it in gradual stages: perhaps starting with one which was only a foot high and then gradually increasing its height.

Rearrangement of rewards
Puzzle out what the rewards are which are keeping the behaviour going. There is a good chance that attention from you will be one of them, even if the attention is only intermittent and takes the form of being cross with the dog (see Chapter 3). There is also a good chance that your attention is not the only reward which is keeping the behaviour going. What the others are will depend on the situation. Harry's excitement in the car was rewarded by the journey continuing, bringing new and exciting sights and sounds. Buddy's cavorting was always followed by an enjoyable outing. Leo was probably rewarded by the reactions of the people in the houses he visited, as well as by the enjoyment of exploring a new environment.

Rearrange matters so that rewards never follow the excited behaviour, but are used to reinforce good calm behaviour. For Harry, Mrs Hamilton achieved this by always stopping the car when he started to bark and only starting up again when he was quiet. In the case of Buddy, Mrs Boyd would first tell him to sit, then take his lead off the peg. As soon as he started to jump about she would put the lead back and completely ignore him. When he had calmed down, she would repeat the procedure. The aim was to teach him that he would be taken for a walk only if he behaved.

In my consultation with Miss Liston, I suggested that when we brought Leo back into the room, we both completely ignore him. When we tried this, Leo was frantic for the first five minutes, yelping, jumping, pawing at our legs and dashing from one to the other in a frantic attempt to attract our attention. He then started to calm down and eventually sat down at Miss Liston's feet. Following my instructions, at this point she patted him and told him he was a good dog.

> Poppy was a springer spaniel who loved visitors. She greeted them with boundless enthusiasm, jumping up, licking their faces and usually urinating on the carpet in her excitement. This was particularly annoying for her owner, Mrs Porteous, who was experienced at handling gun dogs: she had another spaniel, Percy, who behaved impeccably. When she was not distracted, Poppy could do 'downs', 'stays' and all sorts of complicated things. But when there were visitors around, she was deaf to all Mrs Porteous's infuriated commands.

The basic trouble was that Mrs Porteous, like most conventional dog-handlers, relied on establishing a relationship of dominance over her dogs. This dominance meant that her dog's main concern in life was to please her and distractions such as visitors were of secondary importance. But Poppy was one of those dogs to whom the concept of dominance does not seem to mean very much. She showed no sign of trying to dominate either Mrs Porteous or Percy, but she showed no signs of being submissive to them either. She was quite prepared to obey Mrs Porteous's commands when she had nothing better to do and when there was a reward in prospect. The attentions of visitors, however, were a more powerful attraction than anything that Mrs Porteous could offer.

The solution to the problem was to persuade Mrs Porteous to abandon any attempt to dominate Poppy in this situation: she was not to shout more and more loudly and get more and more fierce. Instead, she adopted a quite different approach. Poppy was very fond of a neighbour, Mr Williams, and Mrs Porteous enlisted his help as an accomplice. Mrs Porteous told Poppy to sit and Mr Williams came to the front door. Mrs Porteous then opened the front door so that Poppy could see him. If Poppy got up from her sitting position Mrs Porteous immediately shut the door so that Poppy could no longer see him. If Poppy stayed sitting, Mr Williams came inside towards her, but if she got up he turned around and left the house. The treatment progressed quickly: Poppy soon learned that she could only greet Mr Williams as long as she remained calmly in a sitting position.

The most troublesome part of the proceedings was the training of Mr Williams. As with Mr Young in Chapter 8, who was enlisted to help with the treatment of Freddy, and indeed in common with many willing helpers in dog treatment, he was so keen to be liked by Poppy that he could not bear to turn his back on her. He mirrored the excitement of her greeting in his own: which, of course, is how the whole problem came about in the first place.

General Over-Excitement

Some dogs seem excitable and hyperactive all the time. Rollo in Chapter 1, the red setter who chased cats, Jimmy in Chapter 2, who chewed up the mail, and Major in Chapter 7, who had come to depend on his owner too much, were all dogs like this. They can be a great strain to live with because they react so forcibly to things which would merely interest another dog. They can be noisy and they can be destructive, both to themselves and to their surroundings. They are often thin, despite enormous appetites, and often tireless. Helpful friends often suggest to owners of these dogs that they are not exercising them enough. It is true that when they are not taken out at all they may become even more of a nuisance, but vast amounts of exercise may do no more than barely take the edge off them. Owners may exhaust themselves in a vain effort to tire their dogs.

In many cases there is clearly a genetic element. This behaviour is more common, for example, in Alsatians, Jack Russell terriers and poodles. Some of these dogs may have slight brain damage, the kind of thing that could be caused by an attack of parvo-virus in puppyhood; or malnutrition in the first few weeks of life. Many have had an unsettled early life, being passed from owner to owner. One might argue that this could be a result rather than a cause of their behaviour problem, but the fact that this kind of history seems to occur more frequently in dogs with problems of excitability than in dogs with other kinds of problems (such as aggression) implies that changes of ownership are a cause rather than an effect of disturbance.

Some puppies who are over-excitable gradually calm down, whereas others get worse and worse. Some families find it more difficult to absorb these dogs than others. This is a situation where disturbance in the dog is often mirrored by disturbance in the owner or the family. Stress makes these dogs worse. For most dogs, as for most children, the relationship with their owners/parents is the most important thing in their lives. An upset in this relationship is a potent source of stress, particularly as, compared with adult human beings, they have little control over their situation: they cannot decide to leave, for example. Sustained disruptions of the relationship are especially likely to occur if the owners themselves are under emotional strain or if there is a general upheaval in the family situation.

These comments may seem to have no practical implications, as most owners are already conscious of their own problems; although sometimes it can take a definite problem like the intolerable behaviour of a dog to make a family aware that they need to take stock of their general situation.

> Mr Drummond was a chartered accountant, correct and
> rather pedantic in his manner, who consulted me about
> Daisy, his cocker spaniel. He described the problem
> in a detached and neutral way, much as one might
> describe the malfunction of some domestic appliance:
> a loose connection on the coffee perculator, for example.

Initially, her problem did indeed seem a minor one: she barked when the telephone rang. But I heard this barking when I rang him to change the time of his second appointment. It was high-pitched and continuous: it made conversation extremely difficult. It was punctuated by grunting noises and muffled thuds, presumably as Mr Drummond tried physically to suppress Daisy. Over a few interviews, it became apparent that Daisy's behaviour was significantly disrupting the Drummonds' life. Not only did Daisy bark at the telephone, but she barked at any sudden sound or indeed at any event which disturbed the domestic routine. The Drummonds had virtually given up inviting visitors.

It seemed that it was only in discussion with me that Mr Drummond began to realize the extent of the problem himself. More significantly, in parallel with the difficulty with Daisy, Mr Drummond began to explore a difficulty with his daughter. She was in her twenties and living at home. A 'horsy' person, she had decided views on the handling of Daisy. She felt that her parents were not being strict enough with her. She herself was able to intimidate Daisy into shutting up and doing as she was told. While she was probably correct in her diagnosis, it seemed likely that her intermittent and forceful interactions with Daisy were only confusing the dog and making matters worse.

As with Daisy, it gradually emerged that the Drummonds' problems with their daughter were not confined to arguments over the dog. She objected to their way of doing everything, she shouted, she made scenes and was totally unco-operative about domestic routines. Mr and Mrs Drummond seemed unable either to tolerate her antagonism, to make her toe the line or to insist that she leave home. The couple quarrelled constantly about it, with Mrs Drummond insisting that it was her husband's duty to protect her from his daughter's outrages and Mr Drummond not really seeing how he could do this. In the course of this discussion, he began to realize that the family's first priority was to resolve the crisis in their own relationships. His pedantic detached manner fell away and he became quite upset. We discussed possible sources of help, such as a psychotherapist specializing in families.

This story does not have a satisfying conclusion. Mr Drummond left a message cancelling his next appointment without explanation. He never made further contact. I imagine that once his façade had dropped and he had allowed me to see some of his emotional chaos, he felt unable to face me again. An optimistic theory of what happened next would be that Mr Drummond managed to make some use of the insight gained and turned for help to someone with a more familiar frame of reference: perhaps the local minister. A pessimistic view would be that Mr Drummond could not bear his own and his family's difficulties any further; that things continued as they were, with perhaps the eventual euthanasia of Daisy.

If you have stress and disturbance in your family, obviously you cannot put it right just to order. Having a disturbed dog will not be your primary motive for doing so, anyway. But while the trouble lasts, there are some things you can do to insulate your dog from the effects of the stress.

1. Make his routine as stable as possible. Dogs are less anxious if they know when and how the important things in their day are going to happen: when and by whom they are going to be fed and walked, when they are going to be left alone in the house, when and where they are expected to settle down for the night.

2. Try to reach a policy decision in the household as to what the dog is and is not allowed to do. If one member of the family conveys to the dog the impression that it is all right to jump on the furniture or go into the bedrooms and then another family member shouts at him for doing these same things, this can be stressful. It is perhaps even more stressful if the same person reacts differently at different times.

3. If there are disagreements between family members, try

not to make the dog the focus of.them. He is almost certainly not their primary cause, but can very easily become a convenient embodiment of more general dissatisfactions. For example, a husband might feel unsettled by what he perceives as his wife's lack of emotional control, her tendency to speak and act just as she feels, without regard or consideration for others. He might find it hard to put this unease into words: much easier to object to the dog's constant yapping and chewing things up and to blame her for it.

4. Try not to use the dog too directly as a source of comfort. If you are upset or lonely, it is very tempting to turn to a creature who is a reliable source of affection, perhaps literally to cry on his shoulder. This is a legitimate use of most dogs, but, in certain circumstances, some may find it too much of a strain. Try enjoying your dog's friendship in more indirect ways, such as sharing walks with him, rather than expressing your emotions to him directly.

5. In general, your aim should be to keep your dog's life on as even an emotional keel as possible, avoiding both positive and negative extremes.

The following case illustrates the complex and subtle ways in which personal and family problems can affect the dog; and how, without resolving the basic conflicts, the dog's behaviour can be improved.

> Mrs Imrie and her twenty-year-old son Ian came to consult me about their Alsatian, Ivan. She looked pale, puffy and dishevelled. She talked non-stop in an agitated and incoherent way. Ian looked embarrassed. Ivan's trouble had started a few months before, when he became very restless. This restlessness now took a different annoying form at various times of the day. In the morning, when members of the family prepared to leave for work or school, he circled round and round them, as if trying to prevent them from leaving. When he and Mrs Imrie were left alone together, he tried to follow her everywhere around the house, even into the lavatory. When he was with her, he would dash to

and fro, twining around her legs. If she shouted at
him, he would sit quietly for a moment and then
start again. If she left the house, he would become really
frantic and she usually found some damage done when
she returned. The Venetian blinds had been destroyed
(presumably in his attempts to look for her out of the
window). When everyone was at home in the evening,
Ivan behaved reasonably enough but when they started
to go to bed he became restless again. He would dash
from one bedroom to another. Often he would jump
on and off Ian's bed and try to squeeze between Ian and
the bedhead, which, given his size, was impossible.

I asked if anything had happened around the time of
onset of this strange behaviour which might account for
it. She said that she had left a chip pan on the stove
and it had caught fire. The fire brigade had been called,
several firemen had rushed in and had drenched the
kitchen in water. She thought that had quite upset him.
In my experience, a single dramatic incident like this may
aggravate a behaviour problem which is already present,
but seldom causes one by itself. There was also something
about the detached way in which she described her part in
the fire, as if she did this kind of thing all the time, which
made me wonder whether she was completely well.

When I probed a bit further, she described how she
had recently had a 'breakdown' and had been off work.
She had panic attacks, in which she sweated, her heart
raced and she thought she was going to die. These often
happened in the middle of the night and she would
telephone her GP, who would have to come and talk
her down. He would tell her that she was not having a
heart attack yet. She said she thought that Ivan probably
felt the same kind of panic when he was in one of his
states. Recently, she had been attending group therapy
sessions at the local hospital. She said she had learned
that what she was experiencing during her panic attacks
was the physical affects of a rush of adrenalin, and this
had made the attacks much easier to cope with.

I asked about Ivan's background and early life. They had got him when he was a year old from a family who had neglected him, keeping him tied up all day. Ian, who was fifteen at the time, had been in trouble with the police and was truanting from school: Ivan had been intended as a sort of therapy for Ian. (Here Ian looked even more embarrassed.) The therapy had been outstandingly successful: Ian had been devoted to Ivan and his behaviour had improved dramatically. But, Mrs Imrie complained, lately Ian had been neglecting Ivan. He was out with his friends in the evenings and did not pay Ivan any attention, let alone take him out for walks. At this point, Ian protested that he did attend to Ivan when he was at home and that he took him for long walks at weekends.

It seemed likely that this was the kind of family in which dramas occurred frequently and that I had heard about only a small fraction of them. I doubted whether I had heard about all those relevant to Ivan's agitated state, but I had heard enough to start making a guess about its cause. He had the right background: a restricted early environment and a change of ownership. During the time that Ian was devoted to him and Mrs Imrie was at work, Ivan's life was probably relatively stable and predictable. He was alone during the school day and the rest of the time he was with Ian. As Ian developed other interests and then Mrs Imrie had her breakdown, life became less predictable. He could not be sure when he would have Ian's attention and when he would not. We do not know what was the matter with Mrs Imrie, what was the reason for her panic attacks, but it seemed pretty certain that her behaviour towards Ivan when they were alone together made his agitation worse: that sometimes she would feel sorry for him and cuddle him and sometimes become distraught and shout at him.

My advice to Mrs Imrie and Ian was as follows: I would suggest to their vet that he prescribe a short course of megestrol, to calm Ivan down. I said that I thought that whatever had happened to Ivan in the past, he was perfectly well cared for now and not neglected; he was quite capable of adapting to the reduced amount of attention from Ian that he was now receiving. It was a mistake for Mrs Imrie to suppose that he was feeling panicky like her; he had simply got into a set of bad habits which he would have to unlearn. You may notice that my advice to the Imries did not fully correspond with my private analysis of the problem. I felt that Mrs Imrie's recruitment of Ivan as a fellow sufferer was not helping at all and my primary aim was to persuade her to let go of him psychologically.

As far as the practicalities of dealing with his behaviour were concerned, I told them to make sure that, as far as possible, his overactivity was not rewarded by their attention. They were to make a fuss of him only when he was calm. Two problems needed special attention: his destructiveness when he was left alone and his pestering the Imries at night. The destructiveness might have responded to systematic desensitization by Mrs Imrie to her departure (see the section on separation anxiety later in this chapter), but I did not think that in her present agitated state she was capable of carrying this out. I merely advised her to ignore Ivan as much as possible, especially just before she went out (see same section). The treatment plan for the night consisted of a mixture of systematic desensitization and rearrangement of rewards. The Imries would change some aspects of their bedtime routine: they would leave a light on in the hall and Ian was to swap bedrooms with his brother. I hoped that Ivan would be slightly confused by these arrangements; there was no doubt that he would soon puzzle them out but I hoped that there would be a few days before he got into his full frantic routine again, when there would be slightly more calm behaviour for the family to reward. As far as possible, they were to ignore his pacing and bed-jumping. If it became so physically intrusive that it was impossible to ignore, they could shut him out of the bedroom, but they were to do this quickly and without comment.

Mrs Imrie came on her own for the next appointment. She seemed calmer and she said that Ivan was better. When I enquired about the details of his improvement, she was vague: it was as if she had not really noticed. However, I established that there had been no more episodes of destruction. She seemed more interested in telling me about her group therapy sessions than in talking about Ivan; I hoped that this implied that she was losing interest in him as an alter ego.

My final contact with the family was with Ian on his own. He confirmed that Ivan was improving, but he wanted to expand on an aspect of the situation which so far had only been touched on. He said that his mother nagged him constantly about his neglect of Ivan. He felt guilty about it but what could he do? He went out with his girlfriend in the evenings; he planned to move into a flat with her soon and Ivan would come too. I was not sure how realistic these plans were, nor how Ivan would fare under such a regime. One thing was clear, though: Mrs Imrie was upset by Ian's increasing independence and by his having a girlfriend. She knew she could not expect much support or sympathy if she objected to these developments directly. Using Ivan, however, she had succeeded in making Ian feel guilty. I pointed this out and reiterated my view that the present arrangements for Ivan were perfectly adequate and Ian was fulfilling his obligations towards him. The less he was used as a pawn in family emotional games, the calmer he would become.

Separation Anxiety

Because dogs are pack animals, being separated from the pack can be a source of stress. No dog likes to be left alone in the house, but most will accept the inevitable and go to sleep until their owners return. But some are so upset that they cannot settle down. They may whine and bark; they may mess the floor; they may scrape the paintwork off doors, disembowel cushions, chew table-legs or loose objects left around. Some of these activities seem directed at escaping from the house to follow the owner; others seem to be simply displacement activities. This agitation is most commonly set off when owners go out of the house and leave the dog behind, but it can happen when they shut the dog in the back premises at night. It can also happen when the dog is left in the car: this can be particularly expensive.

Most of the dogs who suffer from separation anxiety get very agitated when their owners prepare to leave, though some have been trained to suppress this agitation. In most cases, the destruction occurs in the first half hour after the owner's departure. More occasionally, it is triggered off by something happening when the owners are out, like letters coming through the letter-box or someone ringing the door-bell. If the owner normally returns home at a regular time, it can also happen just before that time as the dog gets excited in anticipation.

The destructive binges follow different patterns in different dogs. Some dogs always do it: the owner may pop out for five minutes to post a letter and come back to find a newspaper torn to shreds. Others may behave calmly for months and then, seemingly out of the blue, the owner may return to a scene of devastation. Others seem sensitive to departures at particular times of day. It is fairly common for a dog to be tolerant of routine absences, such as the owner going to work, but to be upset if he goes out at an unusual time.

These dogs often put their owners in an agonizing dilemma. They tend to be very loving and responsive dogs: after all, it is their attachment to their owners which is at the root of their problem. On the other hand, some do so much damage that it simply cannot be tolerated. I have come across some owners who have resigned themselves to sitting in a sitting-room with no carpet, on a sofa with its stuffing hanging out, because they know that any furnishings which are replaced will immediately be damaged. But not many people are prepared to live in this kind of way.

Some of these dogs behave normally except when they are left on their own. Others, like Ivan, are generally over-excitable. Separation anxiety symptoms are simply one particular form of agitated behaviour and can be treated by the methods outlined earlier in this chapter. But, after aggression, it is the most common serious behaviour problem and if your dog suffers from it there are some specific suggestions which you may find helpful.

Treatment methods not recommended

1. Owners of these dogs are sometimes advised to confine them in a dog box or small room when they are out, or even to muzzle them. A muzzle can be dangerous (for example if the dog were to vomit) and all these measures are likely to make the dog more desperate. Shutting the dog away somewhere where he can do no damage may be a necessary safeguard in an emergency, but it is not a treatment method.

2. Frequently owners get cross with their dogs and punish them when they come back and discover the damage. They may be encouraged in this moral stance by the dog's guilty manner. Owners often report that their dogs greet them cheerfully, except when they have been destructive: on these occasions they will slink away, as if they knew they had done wrong. As was pointed out in Chapter 2, it makes no sense to attribute this kind of moral awareness to a dog. He has merely learned to associate the combination of the stimuli of the owner's return and of the results of this destructiveness (e.g. the contents of the waste-paper basket scattered around) with impending punishment.

Anyway, regardless of moral considerations, punishment administered so long after the destructive activity could not possibly have any influence upon it and will serve to confuse and stress the dog more.

3. Some owners try being severe with their dogs before they leave: they may deliver a lecture, warning them not to misbehave and taking them on a tour of sites of potential damage. A dog cannot really make sense of all this: it can only serve to make him more frightened and agitated, and therefore even more likely to embark on a destructive binge.

4. Other owners, realizing that their dogs miss them when they are out, may try to compensate them for it by making a fuss of them before they leave. Unfortunately, this only heightens the contrast between the owner's presence and his absence.

5. If the dog is lonely, it might seem sensible to get another one to keep him company. This can work, but if the new dog assumes a subordinate role in relation to the old dog, he may follow his leader and join in the destruction.

Recommended treatment methods
Not all of these methods are suitable for all dogs. You will have to pick out those appropriate to your own situation.

1. Try to reduce the impact of your absence by giving the dog less attention when you are at home. Your aim should be to encourage the dog to develop other interests and make yourself less the centre of his universe. It is particularly important to ignore the dog for the half hour or so before you leave the house.

2. Many of these dogs follow their owners around the house, trying to keep them in view all the time. If your dog is like this, make sure he has a special place of his own, like a basket or bean bag. Reward him for going there on command, always taking the reward to him rather than

rewarding him for jumping out of the basket to get it (Fig. 13) Gradually increase the time he has to stay there in order to qualify for a reward and leave the room yourself for increasing amounts of that time. The aim is to have a dog who can stay in a different room from you without getting upset.

Fig. 13
Teaching a dog to stay in his basket.

3. If your dog gets agitated when you prepare to leave and if he starts his destruction straight after you have gone, try systematically desensitizing him to your departure. First of all, break down your pre-departure routine into its components: picking up your keys, putting on your coat, and so on. Having told the dog to sit in his basket, perform one component repeatedly throughout the day,

without the others and without going out. The dog should learn that if you pick up your handbag, for example, it does not mean that he is going to be left on his own and therefore he should not become agitated when you do this.

When you have desensitized him to all the components separately, gradually put them together. Then, still with the dog in his basket, try out a mini-departure by going out of the door and immediately coming back in again. Hopefully you will find the dog still calm. If so, very gradually increase the length of your absence. Keep a random element in the length of time you are away, so that the dog cannot exactly predict when you will appear: for example, at one stage of your desensitization programme, the lengths of your absences might be ten seconds, then thirty seconds, then fifteen seconds. Because the period just after the owner's departure is usually the critical one, if you can train him to tolerate a half-hour absence, you will probably find that he is safe to leave for much longer, also.

The treatment has a much greater chance of success if the dog is not left alone over the period that this is being carried out. This may be hard to arrange, especially if you go out to work. Arranging for the dog to stay with a minder, or carrying out the treatment during a holiday break, are possible solutions.

4. When you return to the house you should not encourage ecstatic reunions. Insist that the dog sits quietly before you will consent to greet him. If you hear him barking as you approach your house, do not open the door until he stops. This may take some time and patience but it is probably worth it, especially if your dog is destructive shortly before you return home. In this case, you may be inadvertently rewarding it by your return.

5. If your dog is destructive only when he has been left alone for more than about four hours, then he may not be suffering from separation anxiety; he may be bored. It is not reasonable to expect a dog to sleep through that length of absence and when he wakes up he will want to relieve

himself and be generally active. If his destructiveness does not occur around the times of your departure or arrivals, but when he is disturbed by happenings outside, he may be motivated by a desire to defend his territory. In this case, reducing his dominance might help (see Chapter 9).
6. In some cases, a short course of megestrol may be helpful. This should coincide with your behavioural treatment and, by calming the dog down, may facilitate it.

Some of the above treatment methods are complicated and time-consuming, particularly the systematic desensitization. If matters are not at crisis point, it is worth trying out the simpler procedures first, such as paying less attention to the dog. In some cases, this alone is enough to do the trick.

> Mrs Teasdale, a nurse in her twenties, came for advice about her Dobermann, Tommy. When she was out at work, he would get hold of any loose objects lying around (for example books, tapes or cushions) and reduce them to shreds. She knew he did it soon after she left, because on one or two occasions she had come back unexpectedly for something she had forgotten. He showed the standard signs of separation anxiety: agitation before she left and extreme excitement when she returned. Mr Teasdale was a soldier, who had been away for the last few months on a training course, only coming home for odd weekends. He was fond of Tommy, but was quickly losing patience: he said that if this problem was not sorted out by the time his course was over, Tommy would have to go.
> Mrs Teasdale was deeply attached to Tommy and felt that to part with him would be the end of the world. She talked lovingly about all his little ways and on the telephone would announce herself as 'Tommy's Mummy', which I found confusing. For his part, I did not think Tommy quite viewed her as his Mummy: he frequently became sexualy excited during the interviews, as he twined around her chair. On one occasion I drew attention to this but she told me reprovingly that it was just a reflex, caused by his having only one testicle. Such was the power of her nursey manner that for

a moment I believed her and felt quite ashamed of
having mentioned anything so crude.

To treat the problem, I suggested that Mrs Teasdale
systematically desensitize Tommy to her departure, as
described above in 3. I also put it to her that, although
it was natural that she depend on Tommy for company
while her husband was away, the emotional closeness that
had sprung up between them was making him miss her a
great deal when she was out. The remedy was to ignore
him more and encourage him to be independent around
the house. Although the thought of doing this distressed
her, she saw the sense of it. She was also very keen not to
lose Tommy. She carried out this part of the treatment and
the systematic desensitization conscientiously: the results
were good. When she came again, it was with her husband
who was on leave; they reported that Tommy was much
calmer and that there had been no further episodes of
destruction.

In order to prevent a triangular situation from developing, in which Mr Teasdale felt jealous and excluded
from the relationship between Mrs Teasdale and Tommy, I suggested that while he was at home, he take
over Tommy's care, with Mrs Teasdale ignoring Tommy
completely. I think that it was crucial to the long-term
success of the treatment that the Teasdales agreed to do
this. They wanted their relationship to work: in order to
achieve this, Mrs Teasdale was willing to sacrifice her
exclusive relationship with Tommy and Mr Teasdale was
willing to spend time and energy on the dog. If Tommy's
behaviour had been a symptom of major problems in the
marriage, if Mr Teasdale had not really cared how lonely
his wife was when he was away and if Mrs Teasdale had
wanted to make her husband jealous by forming another
relationship, I think the outcome would have been very
different.

11 • *Miscellaneous Problems*

Eating Disorders

Eating is a pleasure shared by dogs and people. Most owners appreciate good food and they like to see their dogs enjoying their meals too. Sharing a snack with your dog can create a special feeling of intimacy: the Christian church taps the same vein of emotion in the ritual of Communion. But feeding does not fit in quite the same way into the lives of the two species. As with social behaviour, there are both similarities and differences between human eating and dog eating: this means that misunderstandings and problems can arise.

Obesity
In affluent societies, obesity is the most common human nutritional problem. The same is true of their dogs: a survey of British dogs found that one in four was overweight. The cause is the same too. In the vast majority of cases, both people and dogs put on weight when they take in more calories than they need. But the reasons for the surplus intake are different. Human beings are omnivorous; they have evolved to eat plants as well as other animals. To take in enough food when eating mainly plants, primitive man had to fill his stomach several times a day. If we fill our stomachs in a similar way, with a modern diet containing a much higher proportion of fats and carbohydrates, we become obese.

Dogs and wolves, on the other hand, are carnivores

who are also opportunistic scavengers. If they are in a pack, they may kill large animals, such as deer, for food. If they are on their own, they will kill smaller animals, such as mice or rabbits. They will also sample anything else they find lying around which smells promising: rotting carcases, faeces, the contents of dustbins. Unlike human beings, they have evolved to feed on a gorge and fast principle. They can eat an enormous meal and then go comfortably for days without any food. Thus many dogs will eat as much as they can every time they are offered a food they like. Such dogs cannot regulate their own food intake. Of course, if their owners do not do it for them, they will become obese. For most dogs, one meal a day is quite adequate. If they are fed more often on a regular basis, they will learn to anticipate these meal times and, if the meal does not materialize, they will become agitated and upset. It will not harm them physically, however.

If you think your dog is overweight, you should first of all consult your vet. He will tell you what weight the dog should be and advise you about a slimming diet. Basically, losing weight is a physical matter: it depends on a reduction in calorie intake. But there are psychological factors which can make this process easier. Many of these are used by organizations like Weight Watchers.

1. Meals should consist of fixed amounts, planned in advance. Your vet will advise you about this. You may decide to give your dog less of his usual food, or to use a commercial diet food. The latter may be the more expensive option but it has the advantage that you can measure the quantities more exactly. If you know that a can should last one day or two days you can keep to that rule: if you depend on measuring amounts of meat and biscuit by eye, there is a danger of these gradually and imperceptibly increasing.

2. There may be occasions, other than the dog's main meal time, when food is part of the social fabric: you and he may share a biscuit at coffee time, for example. To deny

him this treat would be upsetting to you both. There is no need to stop giving him something at this time, but it must be counted in his total daily calorie allowance.

3. Low-calorie, high-fibre foods, such as bran or vegetables, can be offered ad lib. This can be useful for some dogs, those who, for example, would rather get a carrot as a tit-bit than nothing at all.

4. Weigh your dog regularly and record the results on a chart. This will give you some encouragement and will enable you to monitor progress.

Loss of appetite
The commonest cause of loss of appetite is illness. If your dog goes off his food, the first thing to do is to consult your vet. Occasionally, though, a dog may stop eating because of some upset, such as a stay in kennels. One dog in my survey would not eat when his master was away on business: he would not take food from any other member of the family. If this happens and your vet is satisfied that the dog is not ill, try to make the food as tempting as possible. Dogs prefer moist food to dry food, warm food to cold food; they also like smelly food. Many dogs respond to hand-feeding. Alternatively, they may eat if they are left alone with their food, but it should be removed after about ten minutes: food becomes progressively less attractive if it is left around.

Above all, don't panic. Dogs can go for many days without food and stay healthy, provided they have access to water. It is easy to make matters worse by hovering around a dog anxiously, nagging him with food.

Early on in my career as an animal psychologist, I saw a Great Dane, George, who allegedly had not eaten for a month since a stay in kennels. His vet could find nothing wrong with him and he looked fit and healthy, if a bit on the thin side: energetic, bright eyes and glossy coat. His owners, Mr and Mrs Galbraith, a middle-aged couple, looked anxious and much more the worse for wear. I did not see how it was possible for a dog to look so well on literally nothing, so I questioned them more closely about what actually passed his lips. It turned out that he had a passion for compost heaps. This was clearly how he had sustained himself over the last month, but Mr and Mrs Galbraith found his interest so repulsive, even to talk about, that it did not occur to them that it could be a source of food. I asked them how they had tried to persuade him to eat. They repeatedly offered him food, but it seemed to be food, such as ice-cream and cornflakes, which was designed to be attractive to human beings rather than to dogs. If he refused it, they offered it more insistently, even following him if he moved away. To alleviate their worries, they had been giving him vitamin pills, which they had to force down his throat.

Obviously the situation of being fed by the Galbraiths was becoming progressively more and more off-putting for George. When I suggested this to the couple, they became rather prickly, emphasizing that there was no way he would eat, they had tried everything. An awkward atmosphere started to develop in the room. They seemed to be feeling under attack, that I was suggesting that the problem lay with them rather than with George; and, in a sense, so I was. I should have attended to this atmosphere at this point and reassured the Galbraiths that I did not consider what they were doing bad or abnormal: that I was looking for aspects of the situation which were capable of being changed. However, I was so keen to see the fascinating spectacle of George not eating that instead I hurried off to the surgery department. The nurses there gave me a dish of food which they made as tempting as possible: warm, mushy dogfood with a livery-fishy smell.

I went back to the slightly frosty atmosphere of the consulting room. 'Oh, he won't eat *that*', exclaimed Mrs Galbraith when she saw the brown concoction. I put it at my feet. George came over, sniffed it and turned away. 'There!' exclaimed Mrs Galbraith triumphantly. I dabbled my fingers in the food and then, completely ignoring George, I let my hand dangle by my side, wiggling the fingers provocatively. George came over, sniffed them, and licked them. There was a sharp intake of breath from Mrs Galbraith. Still carefully keeping my gaze averted from George, I took a lump of meat out of the dish and held it by my side. George ate it. Silence fell in the room; all pretence of casual conversation was abandoned. I put my hand in the dish and kept it there. George came over, sniffed and began to eat the meat in the dish. I took my hand away and George went on eating until he had licked the dish clean.

I felt terribly pleased with myself. I had proved that George's refusal to eat was dependent on the way the food was presented. But this beautiful demonstration was lost on the Galbraiths. They felt they had been made fools of. Vainly did I try to explain to them that the reasons why George had eaten here were that this was an unfamiliar situation and I was an unfamiliar person, whom he had not learned to associate with food refusal; I had not forced food on him, but had behaved as if I did not care one way or the other; also the food had been designed to be attractive to him, although repulsive to us. The Galbraiths remained polite, but by scraping of chairs and snapping of handbags indicated that their minds were on departure. Afterwards, I wrote a smug letter to the vet, but I did not hear what happened to the dog.

The mistake I made in this consultation was one commonly made by dog-trainers who are trying to help owners. The Galbraiths looked on while I interacted with the dog and the dog behaved in the desired way. One might think that such a demonstration was better than any words, but there are two things wrong with it. Firstly, it is a bit of a cheat: it is much easier to change a dog's behaviour if you are strange to him and he is in strange surroundings. Secondly, by doing what an owner has been unable to do, it is very easy to make him feel incompetent and inferior.

I have found that it is much better to suggest to the owner how he might change his behaviour and to encourage him to try this out.

There are also dogs who do not suddenly lose their appetites: they have never been hearty eaters. Some of these spread a meal over the whole day, eating only a little at a time. Others refuse commercial dog food and insist on high-protein meals of chicken or butcher meat, which have to be specially prepared by the owner. Sometimes, there seems to be a hormonal factor in this faddiness. It is more common in dominant male dogs. Spayed bitches, on the other hand, tend to show the opposite tendency: they may eat anything and everything. In many cases, there is an element of learning, too. A dog who has been rewarded with a dish of chicken or cat food for refusing run-of-the-mill tinned dog food, will be encouraged in his fussiness.

If you have a dog like this, it is to some extent up to you how far you are prepared to indulge his tastes. On the other hand, you should bear in mind that the diet he prefers is not necessarily the diet which is best for him. As a general rule, protein should make up only about twenty per cent of the dry matter of a dog's food: the proportion to be found in reputable commercial dog foods. Most dogs, however, if given the choice, prefer foods like meat or tinned cat food, which have a higher protein content.

If you want to change your dog's diet to a more orthodox one, you have the best chance of success if you do it gradually. Begin by mixing a tiny quantity of dog food in with his chicken; then very gradually increase the proportion.

Perverse appetites
Dogs may eat things which disturb their owners. These substances fall into two classes:
1. Substances which dogs can easily digest, but which are repulsive to their owners, for example, worms, the

contents of dustbins or decaying plant or animal material. What upsets people most is coprophagia: eating faeces, either their own, that of another dog, or that of another species. Unfortunately, they can seldom be persuaded to give this up by rectifying some supposed nutritional deficiency. It is part of a dog's normal behaviour repertoire. A bitch will clean up after her puppies; if she is given the opportunity, she may go on doing this even when they are some months old. Dogs who live in kennels occasionally get into the habit of eating their own faeces, perhaps out of boredom.

If you wish to break your dog of such a habit, the best way to do it is to deny him the opportunity to indulge in it, while rewarding him for doing something else instead. For example, if he does it in parks, keep a close eye on him when you are there and call him if he looks as if this is what is on his mind. Play games with him to keep him distracted. If you are lucky, after a few weeks or months of this you will find that the habit has been broken.

If a dog is eating his own faeces, or that of another dog in the household, it is usually possible to prevent this by clearing up any mess immediately. A problem may arise if the dog is not fully house-trained and if he is left on his own for long periods of time. In this case, the problem of house-training should be addressed first (see section on Inappropriate Urination and Defecation below).

It is also possible to tackle the problem by adding to the situation some unpleasant features which neutralize the rewarding aspects of the habit. Smacking the dog, even if you can catch him in the act, is no good, because he will soon learn that he can safely do it when you are not there. Creeping up on him unawares, with, for example, a bucket of water is better, but he will probably soon learn to watch out for that too. Although you may find the idea too distasteful, a more sophisticated solution is to booby-trap the faeces with a substance which makes the dog feel sick: ask your vet about this. Alternatively, you might try Tabasco sauce. But, as was seen in Chapter 3, punishing bad behaviour is always a less reliable method than rewarding good behaviour.

2. Dogs may eat things, such as pebbles or pieces of rubber or wood, which even they cannot digest. Sometimes this is an unintentional side-effect of chewing. Dogs should not be given toys which can come apart dangerously in this way. Sometimes a dog first swallows a small object when his owner tries to take it away from him; the swallowing may then become a habit. The whole thing may turn into a vicious circle: the dog finds a pebble in the garden; he picks it up and comes indoors with it; when his owners see him with something in his mouth, there is immediate uproar and alarm; there is an exciting and enjoyable chase round the house. The dog finally takes refuge under a chair where someone grabs him and tries to get the pebble away from him: unsuccessfully, because he swallows it. The result is more alarm and concerned attention.

The solution is to ignore the dog when he picks up the stone in the first place. But you should observe him surreptitiously, as he might still swallow it in a bid for attention; in that event, you should consult your vet, or at least make sure that the stone has come out at the other end.

Food stealing

Amazingly, some dogs can be trusted not to steal food: they can safely be left alone with the Sunday joint. No other domestic pet is expected to exercise such restraint. If a cat steals the fish which was intended for supper, most owners will curse themselves for having forgotten to put it away. This feature of the dog's behaviour is linked with his social system. If your dog sees you as dominant, it will make sense to him if you make clear that something is yours and he must not touch it. But if a dog sees himself as dominant over you or if he is a dog to whom the concept of dominance is of little importance, then you may lecture him on this topic until you are blue in the face, but still to no avail: when your back is turned, he will grab what he can.

Some dogs learn to open the refrigerator. They usually find the contents so exciting that, once learned, this trick is never forgotten. The best solution is to fit a catch designed to foil toddlers with the same idea in mind.

Inappropriate Urination and Defecation

Dogs and cats are normally part of the family in a way that other species are not. This intimacy is only possible because dogs and cats have the instinct to urinate and defecate in certain places and to avoid others: they can therefore be house-trained. Pets like rabbits or even budgerigars, who relieve themselves whenever and wherever they feel like it, inevitably place a greater burden of tolerance on owners who allow them to roam freely around the house.

If a dog messes in the house, his owner often feels outraged, as if a tacit agreement had been broken. It is accepted that puppies make 'mistakes'. After all, human children are not expected to behave themselves all the time. But, owners feel, adult dogs know what is expected of them and, unless they are ill, are capable of behaving accordingly. The trouble is that from the dog's point of view there is no 'should' about it. Moral indignation has no place in the treatment of urination or defecation problems and tends to make matters worse. In order to be in a position to take effective action, you have to keep calm and work out why the dog is behaving this way. Dogs may urinate in the house for a number of reasons. Most of these reasons also apply to defecation:

1. *Illness*
A dog may urinate or defecate more frequently because of illness. In the case of urination, this may or may not

be accompanied by excessive drinking. In the case of defecation, it is often accompanied by a change in the consistency of the stools. But if the dog messes in the house only during a particular period of the day and if he can last for six or eight hours at another time without having to go out, this suggests a psychological rather than a physical cause.

2. *Stress and excitement*
In situations of extreme terror, human beings may lose control of bladder or bowels: this can happen to soldiers in battle. The same can happen to dogs when they are frightened. It can also happen when they are very excited: Poppy, the springer spaniel in Chapter 10, was liable to wet the floor when she greeted visitors. Doing anything which increases these dogs' level of arousal, such as smacking them or shouting at them, merely makes things worse. You should try to reduce his level of fear or excitement as described in Chapter 10: either by systematic desensitization or by rearrangement of rewards.

3. *Separation anxiety*
Upset at being separated from his owner may cause a dog to urinate. People often feel this urge before an important occasion. Similarly, a dog who is agitated and restlessly pacing about may need to urinate more frequently than one who is sitting calmly in his basket. Again, punishment merely compounds the problem: the underlying distress at separation must be tackled.

Some dogs mess in the house only when they are shut in the kitchen at night. These dogs are often suffering from some degree of separation anxiety. There is a simple solution but it is not acceptable to many owners: allow the dog into the bedroom. If you are not prepared to take this easy way out you are in for a more difficult time. You will have to treat the problem in the same way as destructiveness in the owner's absence (see Chapter 10): stop all punishment and encourage independence.

In many of these cases there is also a component of faulty learning: the dog may have got into the habit of urinating when he gets restless at night, but he may be capable of learning not to. In other words, it may be worth treating the problem as if it resulted from faulty house-training (see Section 6 below). To do this, you would first of all have to pin-point the time of night at which the dog usually urinates: this might be at a specific time or it might be when he hears someone moving about the house. You should then take preventive action every night by letting him out to urinate before he has a chance to do it in the house. This may mean getting up specially in the middle of the night or it may mean making a rule that anyone who gets up in the night must let the dog out before he urinates. Once this new habit is established, it should be possible gradually to extend the time he can wait before he goes out.

4. *Submissive urination*

Some dogs urinate when they are approached by a person or another dog whom they perceive as extremely dominant. At the same time they usually crouch down in a submissive attitude or role over on their backs with one leg in the air (see Figs 7 and 8 on p. 59). This behaviour is most commonly seen in puppies and usually disappears as they grow older. In the meantime, if your puppy does this when you greet him, try not to approach him in too threatening a manner. Do not look him directly in the eye; crouch down rather than towering above him. Better still, let him come to you.

5. Territorial marking

For some dogs, marking every lamp-post is a favourite recreation. Some bitches have a similar pastime, squatting every few minutes to deposit a drop or two. On walks, this is usually stimulated by the smell of urine marks made by other dogs: there is a compulsion to put one's own stamp on top of these and thus reclaim the territory. Some dogs do it indoors as well. You should suspect a marking element in the urination if there is only a small quantity of urine and if he sometimes does it soon after passing a normal quantity outside.

Dogs may mark in other people's houses, especially if they smell traces of other dogs. They may mark at home, too, if a dog comes to visit. Marking may also be triggered by the presence of a human visitor; this can be embarrassing, especially if the dog deposits the mark on the visitor himself.

Once you have pin-pointed the situations in which it is likely to happen, the problem can usually be coped with by keeping a close eye on the dog at dangerous times. He may have favourite spots for marking, being drawn to them by the smell of previous marks. You should therefore clean up these stains thoroughly, but not with disinfectant: this leaves a distinctive smell of its own which may itself attract dogs. Use bleach on hard surfaces and for soft surfaces use a biological stain remover.

If territorial marking gets out of hand, castration may reduce it in male dogs. It is also worth increasing your dominance over a dog of either sex.

6. *Faulty learning*

Cats are, on the whole, easier to house-train than dogs. Cats normally have an instinct to urinate or defecate on a crumbly surface, one they can dig holes in. When you let them outside as kittens, they automatically use the flower-beds; if you give them a litter tray, they use that.

Dogs, on the other hand, do not have such a strong preference for a particular kind of surface. They have an instinct to use the same kind of place each time, but they have to learn what kind of place that is. They have an instinct to urinate where they smell traces of old urine: this also makes them seek out the same site. As explained in Chapter 3, classical conditioning then comes into play: the act of urination becomes associated with other stimuli in their surroundings, such as grass or gutters.

Any dog, unless his brain is badly damaged, is capable of this learning. But some puppies are easier to house-train than others. A good breeder will make the task easier for you by starting the process early. As soon as a puppy can stagger, at two to three weeks old, he will try to come out of his bed to urinate. His bed should be provided with an easy exit and this should lead on to a suitable surface, one which can also be conveniently used around the house later: newspaper is ideal. By the time he goes to his new home at eight weeks, the puppy should have learned that newspaper is for urinating on, though he will not get it right every time. If the breeder has taken him outside for some urinations, he may also have begun to get that idea, too.

To take up where the breeder has left off, your aim is to arrange that, as far as possible, urination (and, of course, defecation) happens always in the right place and never in the wrong place. This means taking the puppy out whenever urination is likely: after sleep, after meals and about once an hour in between these times. If you pay attention to your puppy's behaviour, you will soon learn to predict when he is about to urinate. Individual behaviour varies, but it usually includes sniffing around for old scent marks (Fig. 14). There is also a characteristic stiffening of the hind legs which indicates that defecation is imminent. This is the time to whisk the puppy outside, preferably to the same place on every occasion, and wait patiently until he performs. At times when you cannot keep your puppy under observation it is wise to confine him in a puppy pen or similar area which is totally covered in newspaper. This ensures that he cannot urinate in the wrong place at these times. Such confinement is also advisable for other reasons: it prevents him from coming to harm or doing damage.

Fig. 14
Puppy preparing to urinate:
sniffing for scent marks.

Of course, you should never punish a puppy for urinating in the wrong place. If you punish him after the event, he will make no sense of this: you will just upset him. If you catch him in the act, he may learn the wrong thing, for instance not to urinate in your presence (see the case of Mr Ross in Chapter 3). If you do discover him urinating indoors, you can distract him by calling his name and then take him quickly outside: but do not make a big scene. It may be easier sometimes just to let him finish and mop up a slightly larger puddle. For human beings, who can learn by understanding rules and principles, the generalisation 'you learn from your mistakes' is true. The same does not apply to dogs. The fewer mistakes they make the better and there is not much to be gained from mistakes when they happen: better for both you and the dog to forget them as soon as possible.

Most dogs go through this learning process as puppies, at varying speeds. But dogs who have been kept in kennels as puppies may never get the chance: owners who acquire them as adults have to do the training then. This is perfectly possible, as long as the owners treat them as puppies and do not expect too much too soon.

All these factors may operate on their own or in combination. In some instances where dogs mess in the house, there may be a single straightforward cause.

> When one of the local vets referred Jinty, a Cavalier King Charles spaniel, to me, he made an uncharacteristic remark. Normally a man of few words who confined himself strictly to the facts, he observed that Jinty's owner, Mrs Jones, had a mind like 'candyfloss'. He would not be drawn any further. The problem was, he said, that Jinty was not 'house-trained'. Mrs Jones, when I met her, looked normal enough, though dressed in a shade of pink reminiscent of candyfloss. She talked brightly about the view from my window and about the other owners she had seen in the clinic waiting room: it was some time before I could pin her down to the topic in hand. She finally agreed that Jinty was indeed not house-trained: in fact, she went 'just anywhere'.
>
> When a dog is urinating or defecating in the house, in order to discover what is causing this, one needs to know exactly when, where and in what circumstances the lapses occur. It was hard to get this information from Mrs Jones. It was not so much that she was reticent as that she had simply not noticed these things. Moreover, she seemed rather to resent the idea that it was now necessary to take notice of them.

I come across this kind of owner quite frequently. They seem to feel that their dogs are rather like the plumbing: that they should fit in unobtrusively with the family's needs and it should not be necessary to go behind the scenes, as it were, and find out how they function. They would as much think of observing their dog's behaviour as they would lift the lid of the cistern just for pleasure and contemplate the lavatory flushing. This is a pity as, even if all goes well, they miss a great deal of the enjoyment of owning a dog.

In Mrs Jones's case, it was possible to piece together enough information to decide that Jinty's problem was due simply to faulty learning. She had come to Mrs Jones from a breeder who had 'run her on': that is, the breeder had kept her past puppyhood in the hope that she had potential for showing. When she failed to come up to expectations, she had been found a home as a pet. But she had lived all her life in a kennel and she had learned to urinate and defecate, not in her sleeping quarters certainly, but anywhere in the run outside. When she came to the Jones's house, she clearly regarded any of it which was not in the immediate vicinity of her basket as being equivalent to the run. She would perform outside if Mrs Jones happened to take her out at the right moment, but she never asked to go out: she had never learned to. She did not relieve herself in Mrs Jones's presence, because she quickly learned that she would be cross; she went away into another room to do it.

I explained to Mrs Jones that in order to treat the problem she must house-train Jinty as she would a puppy. She protested that they had acquired a dog as an adult precisely to avoid having to do this. I commiserated but insisted that this was the only possible approach. As I described what she would have to do, her eyes started to wander and I realized that the vet had been here before me. Remembering the comment about the candyfloss mind, I felt somewhat despairing. I began to see that she was one of those owners who deep down, whether they are consciously aware of it or not, are convinced that I, or the vet, have the ability to dispense a magic pill to remedy the situation, but that we are perversely withholding it. This was confirmed when, with the air of one playing an ace, she announced that they were moving house next week. They were moving to a third-floor flat with no garden. I boggled. How had she imagined she would manage? It had not occurred to her when they bought the flat, she said.

Making the best of a bad job, I commented that the new flat was a good opportunity for Jinty to make a fresh start and learn different habits. But, in order to take advantage of this, she would have to be able to give a great deal of attention to Jinty, supervising her whenever she was on the loose round the flat, to make sure that she made no mistakes. I suggested that it would be worth putting Jinty into kennels over the time of the move until Mrs Jones was in a position to give her that attention. Mrs Jones gave this proposal her full attention: she clearly felt that this was the most sensible thing I had said so far.

She left without making another appointment, saying she would contact me again if she needed to. I felt that she left disappointed, because I had not been able to provide the quick solution she was looking for. Jinty was probably house-trainable, but without commitment on the part of her owner, I doubted if she would ever become house-trained.

In some cases a more complex set of factors is at work.

> Mr Duncan telephoned me in some agitation about his dog Danny. Danny had been urinating in the house and the vet had suggested castration. Mr Duncan had been very upset by this idea, so the vet had told him to seek my opinion. Mr Duncan turned out to be a large man in his thirties, but flabby-looking with an unhealthy pallor. Danny was an attractive black Labrador who bounced forward cheerfully to greet me. His owner jerked him back sharply on his choke chain and gave him a smack. After this rather awkward start, we sat down to discuss the problem. Mr Duncan told me that he ran several discos and amusement arcades. He had to move continuously from one to the other, right round the clock: he was out from ten in the morning until three the next morning, though he would call in at home at intervals. He lived in a tenement flat with his elderly parents. They were fond of the dog, but they were not able to take on any of his care.
> When we tried to discuss the urination difficulty, it became clear that we had a problem. Mr Duncan could find no words to describe the process of urination, nor of defecation, for that matter. This is unusual: in my

experience, owners may use all kinds of vocabulary, ranging from clinical to baby talk (I was once rung up by a woman who asked with great urgency and without preamble why her Bessie would do her 'wids' outside, but her 'tids' inside), but we manage to communicate somehow. For Mr Duncan, though, I had to supply the words. He looked immensely relieved, saying 'Is that what you call it?' Using this new vocabulary, he told me that Danny never defecated in the house, but he urinated copiously, anytime, anywhere. He did not even bother to lift his leg: he just suddenly did it where he stood, without any preliminary sniffing around.

Though Mr Duncan felt himself to be at the mercy of a totally unpredictable phenomenon, there was, in fact, some pattern to it. There were two occasions in the day when Danny urinated regularly. In the morning, it happened after breakfast, just before Mr Duncan took him out: he would discover him trembling and doing it in his food dish. The other time was late at night: after Mr Duncan's parents had gone to bed and before he himself returned at the end of his long day. Danny was left alone in the sitting-room at this time and he always urinated on the rug.

It sounded like a complicated problem with several factors involved. But one thing seemed clear: Danny's urination was not territorial marking. There was therefore no reason to think that castration would help it. When I told Mr Duncan this he again looked pleased and relieved. Some men are unwilling to have their dogs castrated because they feel that this would reflect badly on their own masculine self-image. Mr Duncan did not seem to be like this: he seemed alarmed by the suffering and mutilation he imagined it would involve for Danny.

From the way I saw Mr Duncan yanking at Danny, scolding him and smacking him, I thought it likely that he often lost his temper with him. I approached the subject of punishment extremely delicately, however. Mr Duncan was not being harsh with Danny because he was callous and unfeeling: on the contrary, he did it because he was unable to cope with someone he felt so close to behaving so disgracefully. When gently questioned, he admitted that he did 'lose the rag' with Danny. I left it at this as I did not want to add to his burden of guilt.

I also asked Mr Duncan about Danny's walks: these happened three times a day and Danny was never let off the lead even in the park. The reason for this was that as a puppy he had eaten other dogs' faeces. He had never been allowed to run free since.

There was another interesting episode during our interview. When Danny lunged towards me and Mr Duncan snatched him back yet again, I asked what would happen if he let Danny come to me. He said with some embarrassment, 'He would lick you, probably.' I said that was all right and suggested that he go ahead. Mr Duncan released his hold and Danny leapt forward to greet me. Mr Duncan visibly relaxed: 'A lot of people don't like that,' he said.

I now felt that I could formulate a theory about Danny's urination. He was required to hold on to his urine for comparatively long stretches at a time. This, combined with Mr Duncan's uncertain temper, was probably enough to make him lose control and urinate, sometimes out of anxiety. The breakfast-time episodes exemplified this: he had an overnight full bladder, he was anticipating both Mr Duncan's frightening rage and an exciting outing. In the late-night urinations, there was probably a degree of separation distress. There was also some learning involved, as he did it in the same place each time.

I was able to make some practical suggestions to Mr Duncan as to how he could manage the situation. He could take Danny out first thing in the morning, before his breakfast, for example. Instead of leaving Danny in the sitting-room in the evening, he could leave him in the kitchen with some newspaper. But my chief concern was that Mr Duncan should reduce the stress to which he subjected Danny. It was clear that he judged Danny so harshly because he judged himself harshly. He was so closely identified with Danny and so ashamed about bodily functions that, when Danny liberally dispensed his urine or saliva, Mr Duncan felt as if he himself had been a naughty boy. His nervousness at the beginning of the interview had been due to his expectation that I would treat him as one: that I would tell him that he had been doing all the wrong things with Danny and that Danny/he would have to be castrated.

I had already gone some way towards calming this fear by dismissing the castration notion, discussing the unmentionable in a non-judgmental way and welcoming Danny's slobbery greeting. I tried to build on this foundation by saying that Danny's main problem was that he got fussed. He wanted desperately to please Mr Duncan but he was so bothered that he did exactly the wrong thing. I suggested that Mr Duncan should be easy on Danny and try to make his life as calm and pleasant as possible. I also broached the notion that he might let Danny off the lead in the park.

Mr Duncan went away looking much happier. He came back ten days later, even more cheerful. The curious thing was that the situation had not materially improved. Taking Danny out before breakfast had not prevented him from urinating in the house: he still did it when his lead was produced. In the evening, he hated being shut in the kitchen, so Mr Duncan continued to leave him in the sitting-room where he still urinated. Mr Duncan had allowed Danny off the lead in the park and he had promptly eaten some faeces. But Mr Duncan was not unduly put out by this: he had planned to cover the sitting-room floor in newspaper and to let Danny off the lead in places less frequented by other dogs. He was optimistic that matters would improve. And so it turned out. A further two weeks later, he telephoned to report that Danny had misbehaved himself not at all in the past few days.

Sexual Problems

When human patients consult 'sex therapists', they are usually bothered by an inability to perform the sexual act. Such a deficiency in their dogs does not usually bother owners, unless they are breeders. Ordinary owners are more often troubled by the opposite phenomenon: an excess of sexuality.

Roaming

Some male dogs and bitches on heat have an overwhelming urge to get together: this may drive them to leave their respective home territories to search for each other. It is very hard to keep a dog imprisoned who is bent on escape. There is a good chance that castration or spaying will help this. But you should be sure that the aim of the roaming is sex and not, for example, visiting the local fish and chip shop.

Sexual mounting

It is natural for dogs to try to mount bitches in season. It is also natural for bitches in season to mount each other. Some male dogs keep trying to mount unsuitable canine partners: other male dogs or spayed bitches. Usually the victim objects strenuously and the situation resolves without human intervention. But a dog who is always on the look out for sexual encounters can be an embarrassment. You should try to establish better dominance over him, so that you can effectively call him to you as soon as you see the glint in his eye. If matters are constantly getting out of hand, it is worth considering castration.

Dogs and, more rarely, bitches may develop a habit of mounting inanimate objects, such as a favourite cushion or rug, or human legs or arms. It is a displacement activity: that is, instinctive behaviour performed out of context and prompted by conflict or frustration. So unfortunately the human victims of mounting are frequently visitors: as was seen in Chapter 5, the arrival of visitors can arouse conflicting emotions of territoriality and friendliness. Or the dog may go and look for his cushion to mount when his supper is delayed.

A remedy which may be suggested is castration. This is often helpful, but it may not be necessary. This kind of behaviour does not indicate that the dog is over-sexed. If you can identify the situations which are likely to trigger mounting, it may be possible to pre-empt it by calling the dog and distracting him into some more innocuous activity, like chasing or chewing a toy.

Sometimes the mounting is confined to one particular object: one of my Cavalier King Charles spaniel bitches developed a fascination for a huge blue teddy bear. She would drag him by one ear into a private place and set upon him vigorously. These attachments are often formed in adolescence, when sexuality is more indiscriminate. In these cases, removing the particular object from reach may be all that is needed to solve a problem. Our bitch never showed mounting behaviour again, once we had decided to confiscate the teddy bear.

False pregnancy
Sometimes a bitch behaves as if she is going to have puppies when she is not pregnant. This usually happens about two months after she has been in season, about the time when real puppies would have been born. The bitch may scrabble at newspapers or rugs, as if bed-making. She may even look as if she is in labour. She may adopt small objects like soft toys and treat them as puppies; she may guard imaginary ones. She will frequently produce milk.

All this is normal. Every bitch who comes into season has a similar pattern of hormonal changes, whether she is pregnant or not. For wolves this has a survival value, giving all female members of the pack the urge to help with the care of puppies, even if they are not their own. The preoccupation with imaginary puppies should die away naturally over a few weeks, unless it is rewarded by attention from the owners. If it is too troublesome, for example, if the bitch becomes aggressive while protecting her 'litter', a short course of megestrol is likely to bring her back to normal; you should discuss this with your vet.

Uncontrollable Behaviour on Walks

One of the chief pleasures of owning a dog can be sharing walks with him. But this pleasure can be marred by various problems.

On the lead
There are two kinds of unsatisfactory behaviour on the lead: going too slowly and going too fast. The dogs who go too slowly may actively try to pull their owners in a homeward direction. They may sit down or they may just refuse to go as fast as their owners. It is safe to assume that a dog who is not old, ill or very fat should be energetic enough to enjoy an outing. If a dog is reluctant, there must be something interfering with that enjoyment. It might be a phobia of traffic or crowded streets. This should be desensitized as described in Chapter 10. Another possibility is that the original deterrent has become irrelevant, but a vicious circle has been set up whereby the owner's irritation with the dog's reluctant behaviour has made outings unpleasant for him. This is likely to be the cause if the dog does not show fear of any specific situations when he is out.

To treat this problem, try, if possible, not taking the dog out for any walks: allow him to relieve himself in the garden. After a week or two, he may spontaneously develop a wish to accompany you: you should invite him casually to do so from time to time. Try a departure procedure which is as different as possible from the previous one: try leaving from a different door, for example. The most important thing is not to rush or press him.

If you have a dog who goes too fast and pulls on the lead, you have probably taught him to do this without meaning to. When he pulls you, you probably go faster. There is also the exhilarating sensation of being ahead: of being the leader rather than tamely trotting at your heals. In order to cure this problem, therefore, the reward contingencies must be reversed. As soon as the dog starts to strain at the lead, you should give some command (such as 'Heel'), then immediately afterwards turn through 180 degrees and walk briskly in the opposite direction (Fig 15). The dog will find himself in the position of the follower, retracing

Fig. 15
Teaching a dog
not to pull
on the lead.

his steps. If you carry out this manoeuvre consistently, he should quickly learn that this undesirable event is caused by pulling: that, in order for the outing to proceed, he must walk on a loose lead. The word of command acts as a warning signal: later in the learning process, you should only need to say 'Heel' for the dog to slacken his pace. Over the period that the training is in progress, you should only take him out on the lead when you are prepared to change direction when necessary. In effect, you should not set out with him if you have to reach somewhere by a certain time.

Some owners of pulling dogs find a 'Halti' collar useful. This fits over the dog's head, like a horse's bridle. Its design is based on the theory that, if a dog who is pulling forward is pulled backwards by the neck, he will be stimulated to pull even harder; a dog who is controlled by the head will give up the struggle, because he feels dominated. The collar is available from most large pet shops.

Off the lead
Once off the lead, dogs can get up to a much wider variety of mischief, depending on the opportunities available. Many of the specific problematic activities, such as chasing sheep or joggers, picking fights with other dogs or scavenging, have already been dealt with elsewhere. In many cases, however, the problem is not so much a special interest of the dog's as his unwillingness to accept the owner's decision that a walk is at an end and to come when he is called. A dog who is in this state of mind rarely loses touch with his owner entirely, unless by mistake: he just never comes closer than a certain distance.

The treatment of this difficulty is similar in principle to that for the more specific problematic activities: gain more control over the dog. Call him to you frequently while you are walking and reward him with praise, tit-bits, throwing a ball: whatever he likes best. As he comes towards you, call his name: he will thereby learn to associate this call with the action of coming towards you. Try not to call him as he runs off, if you do not think it likely he will respond; doing this would teach him the opposite: to go further away when you call. When, under this regime, he comes to hand quite readily, put him on the lead as well, letting him off again almost at once. Make the putting on of the lead an orderly performance and one which is pleasant for the dog: do not grab him crossly. For example, when he comes close, tell him to sit, reward and praise him, put on the lead, reward and praise him again.

Of course you should not punish the dog at any stage. Owners commonly make the mistake of being angry with their dogs when they eventually recapture them. This naturally has the effect of deterring them still more from coming to hand.

In an emergency, if you have come to the end of your walk and the dog is refusing to come, the cardinal rule is not to chase him. This immediately puts him in the role of leader and you in the role of follower. Try walking away, even to the extent of getting into the car or preparing to leave the park. Do something interesting, like sitting down and opening a packet of biscuits or stopping to talk to another owner and his dog; or do something unusual, like lying down on the ground. This will often bring him to hand.

Misbehaviour with Visitors

It is common for dogs to make their presence felt when visitors arrive. This is not always a problem. Many owners are reassured when their dog gives a warning bark or are pleased when he runs forward with wagging tail. But there is a fine line between the acceptable and the unacceptable: a dog who will not stop barking or who jumps up on non-dog-lovers is clearly an embarrassment.

Aggression towards visitors is a variant of dominance

aggression and is dealt with on pages 145–6. Over-exuberant greetings are usually the result of learning: the dog is almost always rewarded by some reaction from the visitor, whether it be enthusiasm, disapproval or fright. The solution is to shut the dog away until the visitor has been instructed to ignore him completely. If a visitor is unable or unwilling to comply with this, the dog should stay shut away for the whole of the visit. Occasionally a dog is frightened of visitors: he may run away and hide behind the furniture. It is probably best to ignore this completely and hope that over time the fear will subside and his natural curiosity will prompt him to come out and investigate. Visitors should ignore him: approaching him with friendly noises is liable to scare him off again.

Sometimes it is hard to know what the dog feels about visitors because he behaves in such a peculiar way. This is usually because he does not know himself how he feels: he is in conflict. The conflict may be between aggression and fear, which may show itself in barking or growling, but with the ears back and staying at some distance from the object of his hostility. Because conflicts can give rise to displacement activities, the dog may engage in all kinds of frenetic activities: sexual mounting, chewing, tail chasing.

Whatever display the dog puts on, if there is any aggression in it, the first priority is to deal with that aspect. Aggression should be taken no less seriously because it is mixed with another emotion. Then, as in all situations where the dog is suffering from the effects of conflict, your aim should be to minimize stress. Do not shout at the dog, hit him or make futile grabs at him. Only try to control him if you are sure of succeeding: a lead attached to his collar all the time may help with this. Otherwise, shut him away before you let the visitor in. When you are alone with the dog, you should practise having him sit beside you on command as you open the door. This will make it more likely that he will obey you in the presence of visitors.

12 • *Prevention of Behaviour Problems*

When a dog has to be destroyed because his behaviour is impossible to live with, this is usually much more upsetting for the owners than a euthanasia on medical grounds. It is also particularly tragic, because, in most cases, the problem could have been prevented.

What Breeders Can Do

Selective breeding
Most behaviour problems have an inherited factor. This has been shown experimentally in the case of neurosis. But almost all kinds of problem are more common in some breeds than others, which in itself demonstrates that there must be a genetic contribution. Obviously the contribution is not as great as in the case of physical characteristics like coat colour; other factors such as early and present environment play a large part. By the same token, knowing his pedigree does not make it possible to predict a dog's temperament with the same certainty as his physical appearance. Two neurotic or dominant parents might produce problem-free offspring. But breeders have a responsibility to minimize the risks by breeding only from dogs of good temperament.

Unfortunately, physical beauty is no guarantee of psychological stability. A dog who is impossible to live with can become a champion and sire hundreds of puppies. All he has to do in the show-ring is, while under the close control of an expert handler, refrain from biting the judge and not look terrified out of his wits. For some inherited physical defects, such as hip dysplasia, screening tests have been devised; a dog can be examined by a vet and be certified free of the defect before he or she is used for breeding. It would be extremely difficult to devise a similar test for defects of temperament, if only because so many of them only show up from time to time in specific circumstances.

The breeder, therefore, has to exercise his own discretion as to whether his dog is temperamentally suitable for breeding. To all intents and purposes it is solely a matter for his own conscience whether he does so or not. The beneficial effect of being selective will merely be a reduced probability of behaviour problems, not something for which he can expect to get much credit.

Some breed societies have behaved admirably in this respect. They have openly acknowledged and discussed problems which are typical of the breed: they have made efforts to breed only from dogs who are unaffected, even to the extent of using dogs from abroad. I deliberately give no examples here, as it seems unfair to stigmatize breeds which are improving.

Early environment
The breeder also has a responsibility to rear his puppies in a psychologically beneficial environment. As was discussed in Chapter 6, from three to twelve weeks of age is a crucial time in a puppy's life: during that period he needs to become accustomed to people and to the sights and sounds of domestic life. A puppy needs to spend as much time as possible in the house in human company, not shut away in a kennel.

Also, puppies should not be sold before they are at least eight weeks old. As was seen, again in Chapter 6, if they leave their mother and litter-mates any earlier, their ability to relate socially to other dogs may be impaired.

Relationship with owners

Breeders also should do their best to sell their puppies only to suitable owners. As well as making as sure as they can that the prospective buyer is able and willing to look after a dog, they should also confirm that he knows what he is taking on.

They should also be prepared to provide some form of after-sales service. They are often the first person a new owner turns to when some problem which is not obviously of a veterinary nature (such as a behavioural problem) crops up. Some react defensively when contacted; they are afraid their customers are trying to blame them for what has gone wrong, as indeed they may be. Good breeders, on the other hand, will be primarily concerned for the welfare of their puppies. They will do all they can to help the new owner sort the problem out; if, eventually, the owner does not want to keep the puppy, they will usually take it back, rather than allow it to be destroyed or consigned to an animal shelter.

The fundamental difference between breeders lies in their motivation. Some seek only to make a financial profit: the so-called 'puppy-farmers'. They are concerned to rear and sell as many puppies as possible in the time and space available to them. They therefore have no interest in selective breeding, optimum psychological environments, vetting prospective owners, etc. The primary ambition of other breeders is to produce show winners. Although the parents of litters are carefully chosen, the selection is based on physical criteria. The more litters are born, the better are the chances of a potential champion: 'top' breeders usually rear so many puppies that they cannot give them the individual attention they should ideally have.

For some breeders, the main pleasure is the companionship of their dogs and the enjoyment of the process of breeding. They may be pleased if their dogs win at shows, but this is a secondary aim. Their puppies are like their babies. They remain interested in them after they have been sold and may form an extended network of relationships with previous customers. These people tend to be 'good' breeders, because they are identified with the interests of individual puppies. They tend to breed relatively few litters, in order that they can devote time to them.

What Owners Can Do

Deciding on breed and sex
When you have made up your mind to get a dog, you first need to decide which sex and what breed you want.

As far as sex is concerned, problems of dominance aggression are much more common in male dogs. An owner who wants to minimize that risk should get a female.

Both sexes are also liable to problems more closely connected with their sexuality. Male dogs are more likely to mount people and inanimate objects and to mark territory by urinating on things. They are more liable to roam in search of sexual encounters and have a greater tendency to fight other dogs. Some bitches become more active and excitable when they are in season and may try to roam. A few have false pregnancies. But the main inconvenience of their sexuality is usually not their behaviour; it may be the behaviour they provoke in male dogs: following, trying to mount, even gathering outside the front door. Keeping them away from male dogs to prevent unwanted pregnancies may be a problem. In larger bitches especially, the vaginal discharge may be unacceptably messy. Most owners of bitches solve these problems by spaying.

With regard to breed, the first decision is whether to get a pedigree dog or a mongrel. There is no evidence that pedigree dogs are more or less prone to behavioural problems than mongrels. The advantage of a pedigree puppy is that his adult personality is more predictable than that of a mongrel puppy. Each breed has a typical temperament, although usually this varies more widely than physical appearance, because it has not been selectively bred for so carefully. Of course, if you know the parents of the mongrel, this source of genetic uncertainty is eliminated.

Information about the typical temperament of a breed is not as easy to come by as one might suppose. Books about one particular breed written by lovers of that breed are usually biased. The writer tends to view the object of his affection through rose-coloured spectacles. Also, his life is often so well adapted to his breed's idiosyncrasies that he hardly notices them. He may live happily with a background of constant yapping that would drive ordinary owners mad; or he may almost unconsciously behave towards his dogs in such a dominant way that he stays firmly in control of dogs who would terrorize other households.

Books which are catalogues of all the breeds available can be misleading too. The descriptions of typical temperaments may be drawn from the wording in the official breed standard or the writer may take care not to offend any breed society. Either way, the language tends to bear the same relationship to reality as an estate agent's literature. For example, for 'independent minded' or 'good watchdog' read 'prone to dominance aggression'. Some books are honourable exceptions to this generalization. You can pick these out by glancing through them. They do not deal in vague generalizations such as 'sporting' or 'fearless', whose applications to everyday life are hard to imagine; instead they mention attributes such as 'tends to snap' or 'hard to house-train', which are only too easy to visualize.

Another way of getting information is to talk directly to people who come into contact with dogs all the time: your vet, for example. The opinion of any individual, however, is necessarily subject to some personal bias.

Two American animal behaviourists, Benjamin and Lynette Hart, tried to solve this problem by asking forty-eight vets and forty-eight obedience judges to rate the typical temperament of fifty-six breeds. Each breed was rated by twelve of these 'experts' on thirteen behavioural traits: for example, dominance over owner, excessive barking, ease of house-breaking. Statistical analysis of the results produced a personality profile of each breed. It also showed that these profiles could be summarized by three dimensions: aggressiveness, reactivity (which is similar to neuroticism or excitability) and trainability:

1. Aggressiveness: high; Reactivity: high; Trainability: medium
   Cairn terrier, West Highland white terrier, Scottish terrier, fox terrier, chihuahua, miniature schnauzer, dachshund.
2. Aggressiveness: high; Reactivity: low; Trainability: high
   Alsatian, Dobermann, Rottweiler.
3. Aggressiveness: high; Reactivity: low; Trainability: low
   Husky, Samoyed, Afghan, boxer, chow.
4. Aggressiveness: low; Reactivity: low; Trainability: low
   Bulldog, basset.
5. Aggressiveness: low; Reactivity: low; Trainability: high
   Labrador retriever, golden retriever.
6. Aggressiveness: medium; Reactivity: high; Trainability: high
   Poodle, sheltie, springer spaniel, corgi.
7. Aggressiveness: medium; Reactivity: high; Trainability: low
   Pekinese, Yorkshire terrier, Irish setter, cocker spaniel.

The usefulness of the information just set out is limited because it is so general: more detail is available in the Harts' book (see Further Reading). Its reliability is likely to be greater than the opinion of one person, each rating being the distillation of twelve people's opinions. But it has its limitations. However experienced these vets and judges are, they have not actually lived with all these breeds of dog, although one hopes they take some notice of what owners tell them. What is really needed is a survey of owners.

In addition, one must be careful about generalizing this kind of result from one country to another, as the genetic pools differ somewhat. My own comment on the classification, based on my own biased experience with problem dogs, is that I do not disagree with it; except that I have seen too many neurotic Alsatians to be happy to label them 'low reactivity'. The results also have the drawback for British readers that several popular breeds are omitted, such as Jack Russell terrier, border collie and Cavalier King Charles spaniel. Jack Russell terriers would probably be most appropriately classified as (1), along with the other small terriers, border collies as (6) and Cavalier King Charles spaniels as (7).

When you are choosing a breed of dog, you should not only consider its typical temperament: you must also think about your own personality, life-style and the kind of relationship you want with your dog. As we have already seen, a mis-match here can spell disaster.

Do you want a warm, close, physically affectionate relationship with your dog? Do you want him to be emotionally dependent on you, following you from room to room, constantly wanting pats and cuddles? Do you want to be able automatically to give him what he asks for in the way of walks, games and general interaction without worrying whether this will give him ideas above his station? If this is what you want from a dog, do not get a male dog of any of the breeds rated 'high aggressiveness' above. Also, avoid the breeds bred for guarding: either houses or livestock. Particularly good pets as 'soppy' dogs are the spaniel breeds: an exception is the whole-colour cocker spaniel because of the risk of 'rage syndrome' (see page 146).

If, on the other hand, you want a dog who will maintain a certain emotional distance and will not mind being left alone, and if you are prepared to take some trouble training him and maintaining your dominance over him, a guarding breed or a 'high aggressiveness' breed might be the one for you.

A more difficult question to answer honestly is whether you are likely to subject the dog to emotional stress. If you want him as a comforting companion to see you through a difficult time, such as a bereavement or a divorce, this is a perfectly legitimate desire. But do not get a dog who is unlikely to be able to stand up to these pressures and demands: a poodle or a sheltie, for example. Get a placid breed of dog, like a Labrador. The same applies if you have a noisy and chaotic household: most normal families with three or more children could be so described!

Alsatians and border collies are popular breeds, because of their media coverage: border collies working with sheep and mountain rescue; Alsatians as police dogs; both in obedience trials. But the characteristics which make them such good working dogs can also make them problematic domestic pets: they are extremely alert and responsive, quick to learn, easily bored. You should not keep such a working dog as a pet if you plan to leave him to his own devices. You must be prepared to put in time and effort training and controlling him and giving him something to do.

I am sure that many readers will immediately think of exceptions to the generalizations about temperament which I have just made: that they know placid poodles or savage spaniels. Where the genetics of temperament are concerned, we are dealing with probability rather than certainty.

Choosing a puppy
Unless you have a particular reason not to, it is best to acquire a dog while he is still a puppy: see 'Acquiring an

adult dog' below. You should buy your puppy directly from the person who bred him, not from some intermediary. Pet shops particularly are to be avoided as a source of puppies, however sorry you may feel for them. For one thing, there is usually no way of finding out anything about their antecedents. More importantly, such puppies, already subjected to the upset of leaving home and litter-mates, are living in conditions of psychological deprivation: in a barren cage with inadequate human contact.

From the section 'What the breeder can do' it should be clear that the owner should choose his breeder carefully. A few questions on the telephone like 'Where are your puppies kept?' and 'How many litters do you rear per year?' usually yield the necessary information. A good breeder will not be offended by such enquiries – indeed he will take them as evidence of a responsible attitude on your part. Bad breeders may well be offended, but causing him to slam the phone down on you is as good a way of breaking off the negotiation as any.

Do not agree to buy a puppy you have not seen. Arrange to visit when the puppy is at least six weeks old: the sight of a three-week-old puppy asleep, feeding or even staggering around will not tell you much. An American animal behaviourist, William Campbell, devised a battery of tests for puppies which were supposed to predict their personalities as adults. These tests included making a sudden, loud noise to see how fearful the puppy was; putting him in a strange place and seeing whether he was upset or started to explore; picking him up and seeing whether he struggled. Unfortunately, subsequent research has found very low correlations between performance on these tests and adult temperament. It is therefore probably not worth risking offence to the breeder by carrying out all these procedures.

On the other hand, most vets will tell you that they see some puppies at eight weeks old who behave oddly in the consulting room: puppies who growl and threaten when he tries to handle them or who show extreme fear. Many of these puppies grow up to be problem dogs. So it is worth screening a puppy for gross behavioural abnormalities. Do not buy one which backs away when you approach or shows any sign of aggression, however slight, when you pick him up.

> A young couple, Mr and Mrs Small, brought Sandy, one of their Great Danes, to see me. His problem was extreme nervousness. If anyone in the house raised their voice or dropped something, he would rush trembling into the next room. He sat on Mr Small's knee throughout the interview gazing apprehensively around: an extraordinary sight.
>
> They already had two Great Danes and enjoyed showing them. They had picked Sandy from a litter at eight weeks old for his physical appearance: they had chosen correctly because, in spite of his problem, he had qualified for Crufts. 'But,' said Mrs Small, 'when we went to see the litter, he ran off behind the sofa and wouldn't come out. We did wonder.'

As implied earlier, good breeders will not mind if you ask about the temperament of the puppy's parents, how he has been brought up and so on. But you should also be prepared to be closely questioned yourself: for example, about whether your garden is adequately fenced in, whether you go out to work, the ages of your children and details of your other pets. However irritating it may be to be interrogated about such personal matters, it is evidence of the breeder's concern about his puppies and should not be taken amiss.

Acquiring an adult dog

Sometimes prospective owners want an adult dog rather than a puppy. They hope thereby to avoid messes in the house and destructiveness: they usually want a more sedate dog who will fit in with the household without having to be trained. For some households this is indeed the best option: for elderly people or the disabled, for example.

The problem may be finding an adult dog to fit the bill. Acquiring a dog from an animal shelter has its own pitfalls (see below). Dogs kept by breeders may not have lived as domestic pets; in particular, they may not be house-trained. The new owner may be landed with a more intractable version of the very problem he had planned to avoid.

The best sources of adult dogs are probably ordinary owners who are forced to part with their pets, because of circumstances such as illness, working abroad or an allergy. You must make sure of the previous owner's motives, however. Many owners try to pass on dogs because of behavioural problems.

Acquiring a dog from an animal shelter
If you give a home to a dog from an animal shelter, you have saved him from possible euthanasia. Unfortunately, performing this act of charity may not ensure a happy relationship between you and your pet. Many dogs have found their way into shelters in the first place because of behavioural problems, most of which crop up again in their new homes. Some shelters (such as Wood Green, near Cambridge) screen their dogs carefully. They try to make sure that their dogs will fit in with the households who get them. They do home visits afterwards to make sure all is well. This must reduce the risk of behavioural problems.

Research has shown that, in particular, the problem of destructiveness in the owner's absence is more common in dogs from shelters. This is probably the inevitable result of the separations and changes the dog has been subjected to. If you get a dog from a shelter you should be prepared for this possibility; even if he does not go as far as to chew things up, he may well follow you anxiously from room to room and be upset when you leave him alone. You should therefore get him during a period when you do not have to leave him (when you are on holiday, for example) and be prepared to go through a programme of systematically desensitizing him to your departure (see page 176).

Living with a Puppy

When you first acquire a puppy, you should be prepared to devote a good deal of time and effort to him; this will prove to be a sound investment. You will have a few specific training priorities: house-training, for example, which is dealt with on pages 191–3. In the early weeks, however, your main aim should be to lay the foundations of your puppy's relationship with you, with his domestic surroundings and with the world outside.

He should come to regard you as the centre of his universe: as a source, not only of food, but of affection, comfort and play. Pleasing you should become one of the highest priorities in his life. The more important you are to him, the easier he will be to control and train.

You should also get him into the way of learning to obey simple commands. You should teach him positive actions: to do something rather than not to do something. Puppies, like children, find self-control more difficult than adults. Obviously, one thing he must learn is to come when his name is called. Teach this by the method recommended on page 31. He will often spontaneously run towards you. As he does this, call his name and reward him when he arrives. Praise is usually enough, because reaching you should be a reward in itself. Soon he will come when you call, if he has nothing better to do. Gradually, you will be able to summon him under conditions of greater and greater distraction.

'Sit' is another command which can be successfully taught early on. Most puppies sit quite frequently. You should say 'Sit' when you notice him do this and, if possible, reward him. In this situation, using a tit-bit as a reward usually helps things along: sitting is, in itself, not a very exciting to do. In fact, a tit-bit held at the appropriate angle above the puppy's head can itself manoeuvre him into sitting. Again, once the connection between command and action has been learnt, you should gradually ask him to sit when he is less and less inclined to do so. You should also decrease the frequency and intensity of the reward.

Of course, you will sometimes have to tell him not to do something. You should do this by saying 'No' in a low, growly voice, a voice which stimulates the threat of an adult, dominant dog. At the same time, you should physically stop him doing the forbidden thing: pick him up, remove the chewed tea-towel. Then distract him into some harmless activity, like chasing a ball. There is no need to shout at him, hit him or frighten him out of his wits; although this will probably happen sometimes (for example, if he unexpectedly bites your toes). If these are isolated incidents, they will do the puppy no great harm, but they probably will not teach him much either.

In any case, you should aim to minimize the occasions of wrong-doing. Try to foresee tempting situations before they arise and avoid them.

An important thing which you and your puppy should be learning at this time is how to communicate with each other. He will be observing you closely, learning how to interpret your body language. You should be doing the same for him: learning to predict what he is likely to do next, how he is likely to respond to you.

Around the house

As far as possible, you should establish a regular domestic routine for your puppy. Dogs are creatures of habit: once they have done a thing a few times at a particular time of day, they expect to do the same thing at the same time the next day. You can turn this tendency to your advantage: it helps with house-training, for example, if you take your puppy outside after every meal. As far as possible, do not allow him to do things which you intend to forbid later. If he is not to go on the furniture as an adult, he should not be allowed there as a puppy. Think ahead. A puppy who sits on your knee at meals or begs for food may be charming. A dog who expects to do this is a pest.

The exception to this rule of 'start as you mean to go on' is separation. All the young of higher mammals become distressed when separated from their mothers (or other attachment figure). Experiments with monkeys have shown that if these separations are too long, the babies are permanently damaged: they develop anxious, clinging personalities. The ability to tolerate separations later in life is fostered by an early sense of security: it depends on not being subjected, when young, to separations one cannot cope with.

Puppies, therefore, should not be left alone for long periods. Ideally, this includes night times. Having a puppy in your bedroom may disturb your sleep initially, but most will soon learn to fit in with your sleep rhythms. It also makes house-training easier. There are some people who cannot bear the thought of a dog in their bedrooms, or who are opposed to the idea on principle. They need not worry too much that shutting their puppy in the kitchen for the night will damage him psychologically. This happens to a large proportion of puppies and most grow up without serious behavioural difficulties. On the other hand, if you are undecided about what to do or if you would like to take your puppy to bed with you but feel guilty about it, you can be reassured that, psychologically speaking, this is the better regime.

The puppy should not be subjected to long separations during the day, either. If you go out to work, even part-time, you should make some arrangements for him to have company in your absence. Maybe a neighbour could drop in, or he could spend the time with friends. The point is that most puppies, when they are left alone, will be a bit distressed but will soon settle down to sleep. But they will not sleep for more than an hour or two. When they wake, someone should be there, for various purposes: to take them out to urinate, to stop them getting into mischief and to prevent separation distress. On the other hand, even puppies should become accustomed to short separations. A puppy who has never been left alone and then, as an adult, is suddenly abandoned, even for a short time, is liable to become intensely agitated and even destructive.

The wider world

As was seen in Chapter 6, a puppy should be exposed to a wide variety of people and situations, to prevent him becoming too upset by them later. If you do not have men or women or children in your household, you should make special arrangements for him to meet that kind of person. You should take him on car rides regularly: to begin with, he may have to be caged to prevent him jumping around. As soon as he has been immunized you should start to accustom him to walks on the lead. These should be exciting, pleasant occasions. If he seems reluctant, coax him or even pick him up. Never drag him along. If his reluctance is not quickly overcome, you are probably rushing matters. Leave it for a week or two, then try again.

Later Training

As your dog grows up, you should start to teach him to 'stay' and to walk on a loose lead: behaviour which involves some self-control. Most pet dogs do not need to learn many commands. 'Sit', 'Stay' and 'Heel' (i.e. walking acceptably on a lead) are enough for most purposes. It is better to practise these simple responses frequently than to try to build up a complicated obedience repertoire. Aim to have a training sessions at least once a day, if only for five minutes.

If you are attracted by the idea of training classes, by all means attend one. It can be a good way of motivating owners. But leave if the trainer advocates techniques involving punishment or excessive force: they will be counter-productive. Also do not be tempted to think that if you attend a class every Tuesday, you can forget about your dog for the rest of the week. This is rather like trying to make children good by sending them to Sunday School. It is the moment-to-moment interactions at home which are important. Many dogs who win at obedience trials are difficult to live with.

Prevention of dominance
As explained in Chapters 4 and 9, some dogs need special handling if they are not to become dominant over their owners. This is more likely to be necessary with male dogs. Some show clear signs of dominance as young puppies: you should take care not to acquire one of these. Others make a bid for dominance later on: they may do it around the time of puberty, at about nine months of age or when they become fully mature, at around two years old. The tell-tale signs are described in Chapter 9: leading a more independent life and refusing to obey commands. You should increase your dominance immediately you see any of these signs. The techniques (ignoring the dog's approaches, rewarding only obedience to your commands) are described in Chapter 9.

I hope you will not be so oppressed by the thought of possible pitfalls that you will stop enjoying the dog as a dog. After all, if you wanted a dog who was no trouble at all and never misbehaved himself, you could buy a battery-operated puppy who runs forward when you press one button, back when you press another and barks when you press both at once.

> I rather forgot myself with a client one morning. He had three beautifully trained Alsatians and a fourth who had resisted his influence and was continually leading the others into mischief. The owner left them all in the kitchen each morning and would return to find they had raided the rubbish bin, pulled the dishcloths from their hooks and helped themselves to the dog biscuits. As he droned on and on about the iniquity of

their behaviour, I suddenly had a disturbing shift of perspective. I felt I was engaged in a ridiculous and fragile enterprise; that trying to get dogs to fit in with human values and wishes was like making a clearing in the jungle: that nature was always waiting to rush back in and take over. After my silence, which had accompanied this reverie, I burst out, 'If you left four hippopotamuses in your kitchen you wouldn't expect to come back and find it tidy, would you?' He gazed at me in some astonishment. I pulled myself together and forced myself back into a more helpful frame of mind.

Although it was inappropriate to share this insight with this owner at this point in the consultation, I find that it is a thought worth bearing in mind. When we get a dog, we are allowing a wolf's descendant into our house, even if it is a small, tame one.

Further Reading

General
F. J. Sauter and J. A. Glover, *Behaviour, Development and Training of the Dog: A Primer of Canine Psychology*, (1978, Arco Publishing Company, New York.)
> A detailed account of the history of the dog, puppy psychology, the genetics of dog behaviour and learning theory.

J. P. Scott and J. C. Fuller, *Genetics and Social Behaviour of the Dog*, (1965, University of Chicago Press, Chicago.)
> A first-hand account of some of the most important experiments in the dog psychology field. There is also a clear and readable account of puppy development.

Wolf behaviour
Eric Zimen, *The Wolf*, (1981, Souvenir Press, London.)
> A fascinating and vivid account of the author's work with wolves (see p. 53).

Breeding and puppies
Kay White, *Dog Breeding: A Guide to Mating and Whelping*, (1980, Bartholomew, Edinburgh).
> One of the best books on breeding, from the point of view of bitch and puppy psychology.

Relationship between dog and owner
A. Beck and A. Katcher, *Between Pets and People*, (1983, C. P. Putnam, New York).

Examines what pets (especially dogs) mean to us and the benefits of pet-keeping.

Choosing a puppy
Benjamin and Lynette Hart, *The Perfect Puppy: How to Choose Your Dog by Its Behaviour*, (1988, W. H. Freeman, Oxford).

By American animal behaviourists: profiles of typical breed temperaments (see p. 212), plus advice on how to choose a puppy.

Index

Afghan, 16, 212
aggression: and breed, 212–13; diagnosis, 131–2; and diet, 126–7; between dogs, 60, 88, 120–1, 131–2, 149–53; dominance, 54–62, 106–8, 135–53; and fear, 146; and male dogs, 210; maternal, 87, 201; predatory, 131–5; and owner attitudes, 102–3, 106–8, 110; and puppy choice, 215–16; and territory, 138–9, 145; towards strangers, 145–6; treatment of, 121
Alsatian, 164, 212, 214
anorexia see appetite, loss of
anxiety: in dogs see fear; in owners, 110–11
appetite: loss of, 182–5; perverse, 185–7
attitudes towards dogs, 92–112

babies, attacks on see predatory aggression
barking, 119, 124; in car see excitement, aggression; when left alone see separation anxiety
basset hound, 212
bereavement see loss
biting see aggression
Bowlby, John, 75
boxer, 212
breeders, 84, 89–90, 207–10
breeding: inbreeding, 79; selective, 207–8
breeds, behaviour profiles of,

212–13, 225; see also individual breeds
bulldog, 212

Campbell, William, 215
car, behaviour problems in, 90; car chasing see predatory aggression; destruction in, 173; excitement in, 34, 36–7; see also excitement, aggression
castration, 124–5; and roaming, 200; and sexual behaviour, 200; and territorial marking, 191
cat chasing see predatory aggression
chewing see destructiveness
chihuahua, 212
chow, 212
classical conditioning see conditioning
collie: bearded, 78; border, 146, 213, 214
conditioning: classical, 27–30; and fear, 66; and excitement, 71; and house-training, 191
conflict, 70, 76–8; and visitors, 205–6; see also displacement activities
coprophagia see faeces, eating
corgi, 212
cruelty, 73–4, 104–5

dachshund, 212
Darwin, Charles, 55, 58
defecation, 28, 42; see also house-training, urination